101
Program Development & Motivational Tips for Football Coaches

Brent Eckley

COACHES CHOICE

©2011 Coaches Choice. All rights reserved. Printed in the United States.

No part of this book may be reproduced, stored in a retrieval system, or transmitted, in any form or by any means, electronic, mechanical, photocopying, recording, or otherwise, without the prior permission of Coaches Choice. Throughout this book, the masculine shall be deemed to include the feminine and vice versa.

ISBN: 978-1-60679-139-4
Library of Congress Control Number: 2010940899
Cover design: Brenden Murphy
Book layout: Studio J Art & Design
Front cover photo: ©Louis Lopez/Cal Sport Media/ZUMA Press
Author photo: Bill Battle/*The Missourian* (Washington, MO)

Coaches Choice
P.O. Box 1828
Monterey, CA 93942
www.coacheschoice.com

Dedication

This book is dedicated to my wife, Sherene, and children, Hannah, Emily, Madison, Hillary, and Marquis. My family has always been supportive and involved in my endeavors as a coach.

This book is also dedicated to my brothers, Scott and Darwin, who are five and two years older than me, respectively. One of the main reasons I loved sports, and football in particular, was from being a little kid and watching my "big" brothers play "under the lights" for our high school. I became a fan of our high school teams and my brothers while standing beyond the end zone, watching the action on the field and hearing the roar of the crowd on a Friday night. Later, one of my biggest thrills in sports came from being on the team with one of my "big" brothers.

Finally, this book is dedicated to all of the young men that I have had the privilege to work with. I truly appreciate their commitment to team and to the coach's vision for team. A teenage boy could do many other things instead of lift weights and run 12 months a year and practice two to three hours a day for several months, but these kids keep coming back with an amazing amount of resolve as well as physical and mental toughness. It has been my honor to be called "Coach." Several times each season, I'm literally overcome with pride watching my boys fight through adversity, improve, make the big play, and secure victory—together. These few moments, added together with all the success that former players achieve, convince me that I'm walking in God's purpose for my life. In 16 years as a coach, I have yet to work one single day! Because of the young men I get to work with, it's a joy to go to school every day.

Acknowledgments

The information in this book is a reflection of all the coaches that have been gracious enough to share with me their best ideas. As many of us know, football coaches are the best "borrowers" around, and I am no different. Very little, if any, of the content in this book was originally created by the author. This book is just a sample of the outstanding ideas I've had the opportunity to learn while observing and talking to many of the coaches listed in this book.

I'd like to thank the following, in no particular order, for sharing with me: Hal Mumme, Mike Emendorfer, Eric Thomas, Ben Blank, Jeff Wallace, Dan Robinson, Andrew Coverdale, Cliff Ice, Phil Lite, Gus Malzahn, Ken Leonard, David Yost, Ted LePage, Shawn Jackson, Paul Day, Steve Rampy, Rick Jones, Gregg Nesbitt, Gene Gladstone, Garrett Campbell, Kurt Thompson, Par Pitts, Shannon Currier, Judd Naeger, Patrick Ross, Arlen Pixley, Rick Vernon, and Ed Warriner, among many others.

Also, I'd like to thank the Union High School football staff, both past and present: Brad Julius, Keith Janssen, Gary Vogel, Chris Kelley, Erick Webster, Pat Luck, Nick Kelley, Isaac Arand, George Hinkle, Paul Brake, Chris Janssen, Jake Montalbano, Chris Sperry, and Pat Leicht.

Contents

Dedication 3
Acknowledgments 4

Section 1: The Pre-Season—Get Started Off on the Right Foot 7
    Chapter 1: General Tips and Ideas for Running a Quality Program 9
    Chapter 2: Meet, Bond, and Plan a Course of Action 13
    Chapter 3: Connect With and Recruit Parents 19
    Chapter 4: Tie Your Program to Your Community and Advertise 27
    Chapter 5: Get Your Staff Ready to Manage and Inspire 31

Section 2: The In-Season: Don't Get Overwhelmed—Stay With Your Plan ... 39
    Chapter 6: Do for Others 41
    Chapter 7: Continue to Provide a Framework for Success 43
    Chapter 8: Ideas on How to Help Parents 59
    Chapter 9: Connecting With the Community 63
    Chapter 10: Evaluate and Prepare as a Staff 67

Section 3: The Postseason: Finish Strong—Tie Up All the Loose Ends 73
    Chapter 11: Be Specific and Responsible 75
    Chapter 12: Pay Your Players Back 85
    Chapter 13: Celebrate and Schedule With Parents 95
    Chapter 14: Reflect and Evaluate 101

Section 4: The Off-Season: Get It Going Again 105
    Chapter 15: Build Up and Train Your Next Team 107
    Chapter 16: Educate and Encourage Parents 119
    Chapter 17: Continue to Connect With and Recruit the Community 125
    Chapter 18: Organize and Train Your Staff 129

Section 5: Things to Do All Year Long 135
    Chapter 19: Keys to Maintaining Your Success—It Never Ends 137

About the Author 143

SECTION 1

THE PRE-SEASON: GET STARTED OFF ON THE RIGHT FOOT

The idea of building and developing a high quality program is not new. Any coach, when entering the profession for the first time, feels excited and overwhelmed at the same time. Seasoned veterans of coaching also experience these same feelings. Be careful not to bite off more than you can chew each season or each off-season. Do the most you can with what you have. Strive to do your best and to provide the best opportunity for success for the young people on your team.

1

General Tips and Ideas for Running a Quality Program

Tip #1: Purchase extra T-shirts, and give them out to support people.

Many people help coaches develop high quality programs. As a coach, it's always a great idea to thank these people and show them gratitude. Maintenance workers, buildings and grounds workers, secretaries, administrators, booster club officers, statistics workers, and filmers are all good people to give extra shirts or hats to. Giving T-shirts away makes people feel appreciated, and it helps advertise and promote your program.

It's a good idea to keep track of what sizes the support people wear. Keeping track of sizes helps keep the inventory down, and it makes sure the gift to show your appreciation isn't received as an insult.

Tip #2: Order custom rubber wristbands with a special note on them.

Custom rubber wristbands are a good way to recognize the start of the season, a big game, or even to designate position groups with different colors. The rubber wristband can serve as a great unifying force for a team. It's a good idea to have a seasonal theme printed or embossed on each band. The bands can then be used daily to reinforce the theme chosen for the season. Using the bands helps each player feel like he is part of something special.

The custom rubber wristbands are very affordable when purchased in bulk. In addition to ordering the wristbands for players, the wristbands can be sold to the student body or even the community as a fundraiser.

Tip #3: Order custom carabinders inscribed with the team name or mascot for each team member.

The carabinder is used to symbolize a link to a chain. Many coaches have used the analogy that a team is like a chain. The team is only as strong as its weakest link. Additionally, linking the chain together symbolizes how the team is to link together, to become stronger and more useful than each individual person or link.

Some teams have a "linking up" time before their contests, to hook all of the links together. The "chain" of carabinders can then be placed in a prominent place to be seen during the contest. After the contest, the "chain" can be taken back apart, with each link being given back to each player. Some teams require each player to keep their link with them at all times, to promote team unity. A poem that can be used with the presentation of the links is shown in Figure 1-1. The carabinder links can be purchased in bulk for less than $1.00 each. It is a good idea to have each player, coach, and manager have a link.

The Link

I carry a link in my pocket
A simple reminder to me
Of the fact that I am a team member
No matter where I may be

This little link is not magic
Nor is it a good luck charm
It isn't meant to protect me
From every physical harm
It's simply an understanding
Between my teammates and me

When I put my hand in my pocket
To bring out a coin or a key
The link is there to remind me
Of what a team member should be

It links me to the team
It links me to the school
It is a constant reminder
That there is no place for a fool

So I carry this link in my pocket
To remind me many a time
That a man without conviction
Isn't worth a simple dime

Figure 1-1. The link poem

2

Meet, Bond, and Plan a Course of Action

Tip #4: Meet with each of your players individually.

Meeting with each of your players is beneficial at this time of year. By meeting with each of your players, you can reestablish team and individual goals. You can also continue to develop player roles and expectations. This meeting can help you as the coach find out about any issues that will take away from the team during the season. A sample of a preseason player meeting form is shown in Figure 2-1.

Tip #5: Have a team lock-in.

Having a team lock-in is a great opportunity to foster team-building. The lock-in has several benefits. At the same time, organization is required to make sure the lock-in is a positive for everyone involved.

When planning a lock-in, recruit help from parents. Your team will consume large amounts of food. You will need to get donations of food and money. If you can delegate this responsibility to a parent or a group of parents, it will save you time and headaches. You'll also need help with clean-up.

Activities that can be done at a lock-include video game tournaments. You'll need a lot of projectors and a big space to set them up. A gym is a good idea. Power cords and surge protectors will also need to be secured. Players can bring in their games and game players. Some football teams stripe their helmets during the lock-in. This event is also a good time to have a guest speaker. In addition to the free time activities of playing, schedule time for the kids to do face-to-face interaction in a structured way, to develop a close-knit team.

A word of caution: All staff members need to be involved with the lock-in. Supervision is crucial. A lock-in can be a negative if hazing is allowed. Coaches must educate players on hazing and what type of behavior is acceptable. Coaches are responsible.

Note: The lock-in is a great time to do a team covenant. The players can create this covenant from scratch, or you, as the coach, can provide samples. Each position group could come up with a covenant and then have the leaders combine the separate covenants into one team covenant. The team covenant should tell other people what the team stands for and what the team wants to be known for. This covenant can be put on a large piece of material and then signed by each player present.

Pre-Season Team Meeting

How to Improve
- Focused mind and body
- Consistent effort
- Feedback
- Encouragement
- Consequences

Why Will We Win?
What Makes Us Special?
- Work harder
- Work smarter
- Work longer
- Better athletes
- Better coaches
- Better schemes
- Better conditioned
- Better leaders
- More committment
- More discipline

What We Need to Do to Win: Offense
- + in turnover margin
- + in number of plays differential
- Run effectively
- Avoid penalties
- Great pass protectors
- Catch consistently
- Great route runners
- Healthy
- Fresh legs
- Conditioning

What We Need to Do to Win: Defense
- + in turnover margin
- + in number of plays differential
- Tackle consistently
- Get off blocks
- Great blitzers
- Zero passing touchdowns
- Pursue
- Stop the run + 2.5
- Avoid penalties
- Healthy
- Fresh legs

Leaders
- Best workers
- Most committed
- Positive
- Unselfish
- Help others

Who Is Going to Outwork Me Today?

Discussion Points
- Why do you play football?
- Define trust.
- Players are responsible for their equipment. Helmets should always be on and strapped. Be ready to play.
- Travel quietly. No talking. Arrive early, dressed in team shirt and nice pants. No jokes. Concentrate on the game and your job at hand; think about being successful.
- Links should be on at all times.
- Regarding academics, sit in the front, arrive early and prepared, and don't be a jerk. Listen with eyes and ears, ask for help, and don't entertain.
- You are special and tough.
- At Thursday practices, think game situations, focus, no mental errors, low contact. Confidence comes from execution on Thursdays. After practice, be ready to work quickly: to quiz, to equipment checks, to uniform checkout, to itinerary, to video, to dinner.
- Don't leave football papers lying around. Take care of yours, and take care of your buddy's.
- Team shirts cost money; keep track of them.
- Check your pads and helmets every other day for issues.
- What makes good leaders?
- You control your effort and how you react to adversity, which are the two biggest keys to success in football and life.
- Unity is achieved when great teams all pull in the same direction.
- Find something to do that the community would be proud of.
- Always jog on and off the field.
- Burn the boats. All is left behind. Do it here and now.
- Are you a team of destiny?
- Dominant teams play great defense and special teams
- Don't miss football practice for a detention or Saturday school.
- Schedule doctor appointments so as to not miss football time.
- Freshman year is a big adjustment year. You can do it; you have to be disciplined, and make the most of your time.
- You have the hardest working coaches in the conference, district, and state. Are you the hardest working team?
- Great teams play with great effort (e.g., pursuit, block to the whistle, etc.).
- The roles of everyone are appreciated. You're all equal as teammates. Not everyone is a star, but we're all in it together, and everyone has a job.
- Uniforms create a singular identity and unity and ensure the team all looks the same.
- Don't talk to officials except "Yes sir," and "No sir."
- Don't talk to opponents. Let your play do the talking.

Figure 2-1. Sample preseason player meeting form

Tip #6: Have your players participate in a daytime team camp.

In many areas of the United States, high schools are able to host team camps. Anywhere from 4 to 24 teams will get together and scrimmage against each other. Many times, these camps are day camps, so the teams will show up at a specific school, play three or four scrimmages, and then return to their own school. The individual state's athletic governing body must sanction the camp.

The preseason is a great time to compete against other schools as preparation for in-season games, and a daytime team camp is one of the best ways to evaluate and develop talent. As you prepare for the camp, it's a good idea to have a list of objectives for the camp, not just winning or playing well. For example, as a football coach, you may want to work on your play-action passing game or a specific coverage adjustment that you want to use extensively during the season. Many times, a team can gain experience equivalent to three or four games from going to a team camp.

Another great advantage to taking a team to a daytime camp is the minimal cost. When going to a college or university camp, the cost can be quite high.

Tip #7: Take your players away to an overnight team camp.

The overnight team camp is similar to a lock-in. Coaches will need to be very careful with player supervision. When going to an overnight team camp, money is paid up front with food and lodging being provided. Again, the overnight team camp allows for players to spend two or three days together as a team. The same rules should apply as to the list of objectives for the team camp. The head coach will need to have copies of proof of insurance and signed waiver forms to be released from liability.

The benefit that the overnight camp has over the daytime camp is the team building and team bonding that can result. An overnight team camp provides many opportunities to create teambuilding activities. Overnight camp can be a great opportunity to develop and train leaders, as well as a great time to develop seasonal themes. Many times, the amount of plays is fairly equal between the two camps. The downside to the overnight camp is the expense. Some players simply will not be able to afford to go to the overnight camp without fundraising ahead of time.

Tip #8: Take your players to a campground for your own team camp.

Taking your players to a campground for camp is a great way to provide intense focus on football and the upcoming season as well as team-building activities. Supervision is a priority. Similar to a lock-in, recruiting help for food and other day-to-day needs is very important. The campground will need to be scouted out ahead of time and reserved. In addition, the campground area will need to be marked for play.

This approach is an excellent way to teach a new scheme of offense or defense. The time away allows the coach the opportunity to schedule team activities all day long. A coach could schedule several practices each day, which would allow for more in-depth teaching at a more relaxed pace.

The cost would be less than going to an overnight team camp at a college or university. Many teambuilding opportunities would exist, and you would also have plenty of time to develop and train leaders. This time would also be excellent for developing a seasonal theme. One negative of having camp at a campground would be the lack of competition against other teams.

Tip #9: Develop a seasonal theme.

Developing a theme for each season is a great way to build ownership by players into the program. The theme is a good way to teach important life skills. In addition to the seasonal theme, it's a good idea to put the theme on a T-shirt or link or wristband. The theme can also be coded so that only your team knows what it means. This aspect helps the team members feel special. The coding could be a translation into another language, using the first letter from each word of the theme, or any other way you can come up with to make it for just your team. Some theme ideas include the following:

- Destiny
- Burn the boats
- Crossroads
- In it to win it
- Work to win
- Turn the page
- Our story
- Finish
- Synergy
- Chart the course
- Zeroed in

- I'm all in
- Pressing on
- Sold out
- Focus
- Get it done
- In the crosshairs
- Taking hold
- Finish
- Make it happen
- We can
- Hold the rope

- No excuses
- 212 degrees
- Fists not fingers
- Unyielding
- I can't—We can
- WIN: What's important now?
- The future is now
- Relentless
- All for one
- Reloaded

- Another level
- Dreaming big
- Go fast, go alone—go far, go together
- 100 percent
- Taking aim
- Us
- We are one
- Every play, every day

Tip #10: Have a memento representing each senior athlete placed in a prominent, visible spot in your stadium.

This is a great way to honor seniors and develop tradition. The mementos could be purchased or made by parents or the coaching staff. These mementos could be a poster, a sports figure, mascot, or a ball. One idea is to have a 3-by-4-foot sheet of plywood pained in school colors and cut into the shape of a football, with the name of the senior player in the center of the plywood football. There would be a football for each senior player. The plywood footballs could then be placed in the stadium, where any spectator would see.

3

Connect With and Recruit Parents

Tip #11: Develop a team policy in addition to the school citizenship policy for athletes.

By developing a team policy handbook, the coach is able to deal with negative behavior in a proactive way. Many high school students are relieved to see limitations to their behavior in a team policy handbook. The vast majority of parents appreciate a coach that has high expectations for players, their behavior, and their grades.

The team policy handbook can communicate to players and parents discipline procedures, fundraising, playing time, practice schedules, game schedules, overall coaching philosophy, and day-to-day procedures. By developing the team policy handbook, the coach answers a lot of questions by the parents of any new players. The following topics may be covered in a team policy handbook:

- Academics
  - ✓ Keys for success
  - ✓ School behavior
- Relationships
  - ✓ Coaches
  - ✓ Other players
- Priorities
- Schedules
  - ✓ Daily schedule from the first day of practice through the first game
- Philosophy
- Expectations
  - ✓ School
  - ✓ Practice field
  - ✓ Travel
  - ✓ Away from the team
- Contract
  - ✓ Get player and parent signatures for the handbook

Tip #12: Develop a practice plan sheet that has built-in routine.

A great way to get the most out of your players as well as receiving cooperation from parents is to have a routine to practice. The head coach is responsible for the entire program, and in turn the head coach is in charge of the beginning and the ending of each practice. Having a regular start and end time for each practice day every week helps the players and parents get into a routine, which will help to improve the performance by players and coaches alike. The program will be more efficient at practice. Players will practice more confidently, knowing what to expect each day before they take the practice field. Sample practice schedules for a four-practice week are shown in Figures 3-1 through 3-4.

In addition to developing the routine within the practice schedule, it's a good idea to make a plan of the practices in the preseason. This planning ahead saves the coach valuable time during the season, and it is always easier to plan out practice routines when not focusing on a particular opponent.

Tip #13: Have a father-son outing.

The father-son outing could be an overnight trip, a lock-in, a day fishing trip, or anything else you can think of to bring the boys and the dads together. It's very important when setting up the father-son outing to have an agenda, a set of procedures, and a list of goals and activities. Remember: supervision and organization are key. In some areas, dads are non-existent. If that is the case, allow the boys to bring grandfathers, uncles, ministers, big brothers, or even use coaches as the father figure. When dealing with non-fathers, make sure to make the expectations clear. Always remember, the head coach is responsible for safety and supervision. Everything that goes on at the father-son outing should be positive and wholesome. Again, as the head coach, you are responsible for everything that goes on, whether you are on campus or 1,000 miles away.

In addition to connecting with the dads of your players, the father-son outing helps foster a connection between the boys and their dads. This opportunity for connection might be the best gift you can give a dad. The father-son outing is also a great opportunity to continue to sell your vision for the program and to help recruit dads to help.

Sample Day 1 Practice Schedule	**Date:** Monday, 9/22/XX **Dress:** Shells **Team:** HHS **Practice:** #40	
Time Per Schedule 3:15 1 Pre-practice defense assign align 3:30 4 Pride 3:45 7 Team offense sit-third down 4:00 10 Individual defense 4:20 15 Team defense 4:35 18 Water 4:40 19 Individual offense 5:55 22 7-on-7 or ROA 5:05 24 Specials 5:10 26 Team offense script 5:20 28 Tackling technique open field 5:30 30 Conditioning 5:40 32 Scouting report 6:15 EOP	**Offensive Periods** Mesh/Killer ROA/7-on-7 Team Four-minute Third down Specials Script	**Defensive Periods** Tackling Pursuit Cage or war Pursuit Assignments on a line
	Pride Preparation PAT/FG Punt-return block	
Defensive Individual and Notes Review	**Offensive Individual and Notes** Notes: • Formations • Motions Specials: • 3 right/left h/y Falcon • Trap vs. even run to 1-5 • Versus odd mash and regular	

Figure 3-1. Sample practice 1 of a four-practice week for football

	Sample Day 2 **Practice Schedule**		**Date:** Tuesday, 9/23/XX **Dress:** Full **Team:** HHS **Practice:** #41	
Time	**Per**	**Schedule**	**Offensive Periods**	**Defensive Periods**
3:05	1	Film	Mesh/Killer	Tackling
3:30	6	Pre-practice	ROA/7-on-7	Turnover
3:40	8	Dynamic warm-up	Team	Pursuit
3:45	9	Pride	Inside	Team
4:00	12	Tackling eye-opener	Script	Goal line
4:10	14	Turnover	Red zone	Option
4:20	16	Individual defense	Goal line	
4:35	19	Inside/7-on-7 or recognition	Two-minute	
4:45	21	Team defense		
5:00	24	Water	**Pride Preparation**	
5:05	25	Two-minute period	Punt	
5:15	27	Individual	Kickoff	
5:30	30	7-on-7		
5:45	33	Inside drill		
5:55	35	Team 11-on-11 situation, red zone, goal line	**Offensive Individual and Notes** Notes:	
6:15	39	Conditioning, champ: second-level blocking/fits	• Formations • Motions	
6:25	41	EOP	Specials: • Quarterback drops, walkback, circle, backpedal	

Defensive Individual and Notes
Review

Figure 3-2. Sample practice 2 of a four-practice week for football

Sample Day 3 Practice Schedule			Date: Wednesday, 9/24/XX Dress: Shells Team: HHS Practice: #42	
Time	**Per**	**Schedule**	**Offensive Periods**	**Defensive Periods**
3:05	1	Film	Mesh/Killer	Tackling
3:30	6	Pre-practice	ROA/7-on-7	Turnover
3:40	8	Dynamic warm-up	Team	7-on-7
3:45	9	Pride	Screen	Team
4:00	12	Jaguar or war	Third down	Red zone
4:10	14	Blitz period/recognition back eight or routes	Coming out Script	Third down Coming out
4:25	17	Team defense		
4:45	21	Water	**Pride Preparation**	
4:50	22	Specials or script, script on air	Kickoff return	
5:00	24	Killer/bubble	Punt block/return	
5:10	26	7-on-7 or ROA	Kickoff	
5:20	28	Screen drill		
5:30	30	Team 11-on-11 situation, third down, coming out	**Offensive Individual and Notes** Notes:	
5:45	33	Championship drills, 1-on-1	• Formations	
5:55	35	EOP	• Motions Specials: • •	

Defensive Individual and Notes
Review

Figure 3-3. Sample practice 3 of a four-practice week for football

	Sample Day 4 **Practice Schedule**		**Date:** Thursday, 9/25/XX **Dress:** Shells **Team:** HHS **Practice:** #43	
Time	**Per**	**Schedule**	**Offensive Periods**	**Defensive Periods**
3:05	1	Kicking warm-up	Team	Tackling
3:15	3	Passing warm-up	Two-minute	Team
3:25	5	Dynamic warm-up	Third down	Two-minute
3:35	7	Script	Red zone	Four-minute
4:05	13	Water	Specials	
4:10	14	Two-minute defense	Script	
4:20	16	Team defense	Victory	
4:30	20	Water		
4:35	21	Offense: Script, specials, all looks	**Pride Preparation**	
4:55	26	EOP guest kicker	All scripted	
5:20		Tests, itinerary, stickers		
5:50		Highlight video		
6:15		Team meal		

Specials and Notes
Notes:
- Formations
- Motions

Specials:
-
-

Thursday Script
First kickoff return (+40)
First offense (-40): Run play and score
First PAT team (+3)
First kickoff (-40)
First defense (+20): Hold on third down
First punt block (+25)
Second offense (-40): Run play on third down
First punt team (-45)
First defense (+2): Safety
First kickoff return after a safety (+25)
First offense (-35): Run play to (+10) just before half
First field goal team (+10): Clock
First kickoff (-40): Surprise onside
First offense (+40): Run a play on third down
First punt team (+35): Pooch
First offense (-5): Take a safety
First kickoff team after a safety (-25): Fumble
Second offense (-3): Run a play on third down
First punt team (-3)
Second defense (+45): Stops offense on third down
First punt block (+40): Block and score
First PAT team (+3)
First hands team (+40)
First offense (+45): Victory
First prevent defense (+40)

Figure 3-4. Sample practice 4 of a four-practice week for football

Tip #14: Have a player-parent float trip.

The player-parent float trip is a good way to connect with the parents in your program. Like the father-son outing, it is important to have an agenda, a set of procedures, and a list of goals and activities. Make sure all parents, coaches, and adults are aware of the importance of being a positive role model for the kids on this trip. The float trip could be a day trip or an overnight trip. If a float trip is not possible in your area, think of similar activities that provide the same type of structure.

The positives are many. Connecting with and recruiting parents, selling your vision, helping children connect with their parents, and overall teambuilding are some of the best things about a float trip. As with any of these player-parent activities, it's a good idea to delegate responsibilities to assistant coaches. Allow assistant coaches to make presentations on the theme or any team-building activities.

Tip #15: Have a team-family picnic.

The team-family picnic is a great way to introduce yourself and your coaches to the parents of your players. This event is a great time for the parents to connect with each other. The more opportunities the parents have to bond, the more the parents will identify with your program. This picnic is also another great opportunity to be accessible to the parents.

Food can be provided by local donations or it can be done potluck style. Some programs assign each grade level with a different part of the meal.

Topics to cover at a preseason team-family picnic could include: practice schedules, weekly schedules, policies and procedures, expectations, contact information, game schedules, and lower-level program game and practice schedules.

4

Tie Your Program to Your Community and Advertise

Tip #16: Provide camps for the youth of your community, and have your high school players teach and coach at the camp.

Youth camps are a great way to be accessible to the community and your future players. By running a youth camp, parents get an opportunity to see the head coach in action.

These camps provide an excellent time to teach techniques and schemes that you employ at your level. The youth players of today are the high school players of tomorrow.

It is important to have the high school kids attend and be actively involved in teaching at the youth camp. Teaching the techniques helps the players increase their level of knowledge of your offense or defense. It provides role modeling for the youth players. The bond between the high school players and the youth players is strong and long-lasting. Take advantage of these very important teachable moments to make a difference in the lives of our youth, both the high school players and the younger players.

Make sure to have T-shirts for the camp. They provide another way to advertise your program and have the youth players feel like they are a part of your program.

Tip #17: Auction a sideline pass for each home game.

This auction is a fundraising idea, but the money is not as important as the access to your program and the advertising for your program. The money could also be given to a charity or to a specific school need, like purchasing books for an elementary school library or classroom.

The preseason is a good time to auction off the sideline passes. The community will already be aware of the program and that the season is approaching, but the coaches will not be consumed with game plans and watching film.

Tip #18: Create a game program.

The program can be sold or given away at games. The game program can include graphics, rosters, pictures, records, past statistics, and a history of the program. This program is a great way to brag to the community on your kids and program.

Programs can also be a solid fundraiser. Sell advertising space in the game program to local businesses. The sales can be a responsibility of the players, the coaching staff, or the head coach. Figure 4-1 illustrates a sample letter to send to businesses, offering the advertising opportunity.

Anywhere High School
c/o John Coach, head football coach
1 High School Drive
Anywhere, USA 12345

Dear Valued Business Member,

Thanks to you, the first edition of our *Fall Sports Program* was a great success. We are now starting to work on our second edition. The *Fall Sports Program* is used to help provide improvements for our facilities, repairs and updates for our equipment, and to improve the overall experience for each student athlete involved in a fall sport. Our football team uses the advertising dollars as a major fundraiser for our program. The other fall activities benefit from having more publicity for their programs.

The 20XX edition of the game program will be approximately 36 pages of photos, schedules, and rosters of all of our fall activities, football statistics, records, and more. Advertising in our program not only contributes to the success of our fall sports teams, but is also an opportunity for your advertising dollars to reach many local and surrounding area patrons. The programs will be available at all home athletic contests.

We are enclosing our advertising price list for your consideration, as well as our 20XX varsity football game schedule with the hope that you will come out to the stadium and cheer for our team.

If you can help, please include a photo-ready copy or computer disk of your black-and-white advertisement together with your check payable to Anywhere High School and mail them to:

Anywhere High School
Attn: John Coach
P.O. Box 1
Anywhere, USA 12345

We will also be happy to stop by and pick up your advertisement. You can call John Coach at 555-999-5555. You may also email your advertisement to jcoach@anywhere.edu. Our deadline to submit your ad is July 1, 20XX.

We hope that you will consider advertising in the 20XX Anywhere High School *Fall Sports Program* and help us celebrate our athletic excellence at Anywhere High School.

In Appreciation,

John Coach

Figure 4-1. Sample program advertising letter

5

Get Your Staff Ready to Manage and Inspire

Tip #19: Create a drill book for each position.

The drill book should include teaching progressions for each skill for each position. To go along with the drill book, it will be very useful to develop a catalog of drills on video for new coaches to use as a reference to learn the primary drills used by your program. A sample of a drill progression is shown in Figure 5-1.

Tackling Progression
- One-knee tackle
  - ✓ Elbow bent
  - ✓ Pop chest
  - ✓ Club up
- Two-knee tackle
  - ✓ Dig toes in
  - ✓ Pop chest
  - ✓ Club up
  - ✓ Extend hips
- Three-step shimmy tackle
  - ✓ Eyes
  - ✓ Shimmy
  - ✓ Pop chest
  - ✓ Club up
  - ✓ Grab cloth
  - ✓ Run feet
- Run and three-step shimmy tackle
  - ✓ Run
  - ✓ Eyes
  - ✓ Shimmy
  - ✓ Pop chest
  - ✓ Club up
  - ✓ Grab cloth
  - ✓ Run feet
- Angle shimmy tackle
  - ✓ Run
  - ✓ Eyes
  - ✓ Shimmy
  - ✓ Pop chest
  - ✓ Club up
  - ✓ Grab cloth
  - ✓ Run feet
- Open field tackle, five-yard width
  - ✓ Compete
  - ✓ Put it all together
- Goal line tackle, five-yard angle
  - ✓ Compete
  - ✓ Angle

Figure 5-1. Sample drill progression for tackling

Tip #20: Create a game plan sheet for each upcoming opponent.

Included in this game plan sheet should be a perfect scenario and a flawed scenario for which adjustments will need to be made. The possible adjustments should be listed. By working on the game plan in the preseason, the coach will save valuable in-season time. Figures 5-2 through 5-5 show sample game plan sheets and opening scripts.

Tip #21: Take your staff away for preparation.

Many successful coaches gather their staff members together for preparation and bonding in the preseason. The preseason is an important time to get final staff input on responsibilities, drills, and routines. It is also a key time to get all staff members on the same page. Some coaching staffs take time away weeks before the upcoming season. The coaches will spend time together at a timeshare or condo. A good idea is to set aside at least two days to go over all schemes as well as philosophies about all that pertains to the sport and the team.

This retreat is a great time to develop preseason and in-season practice schedules. This time can also be used as a mini-clinic for any new coaches, or the time can be spent to teach all coaches new techniques to focus on in the upcoming season. This time is also good to use as staff development and have coaches practice teaching the drill progressions and schemes to each other. Coaches can also use this time to put together lessons for preseason camps as well as developing lessons on the seasonal theme, team-building lessons, or character education.

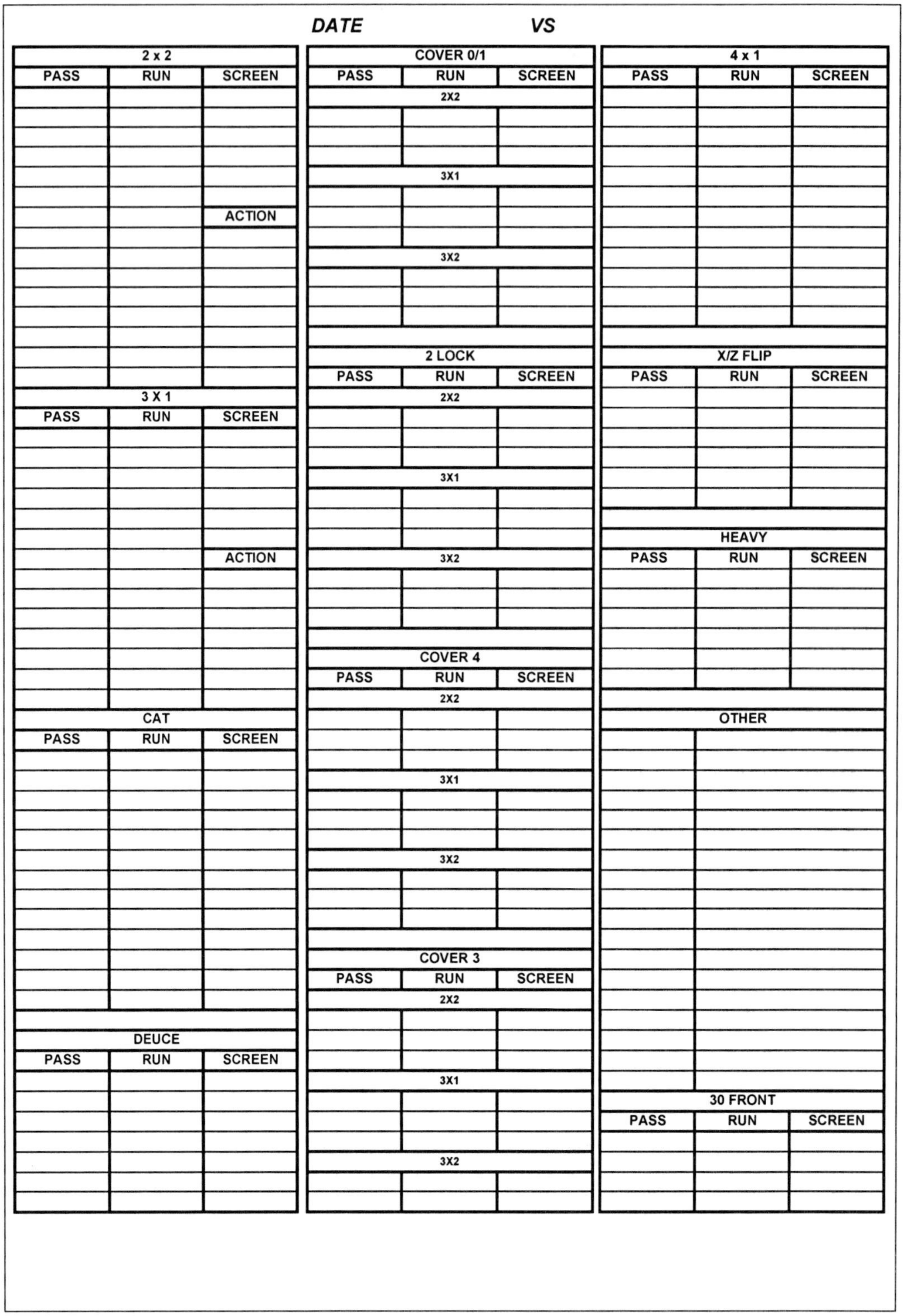

Figure 5-2. Sample offensive game plan sheet by formation

SCRIPT			
LEFT HASH			**RIGHT HASH**
	1		
	2		
	3		
	4		
	5		
	6		
	7		
	8		
	9		
	10		
	11		
	12		
	13		
	14		
	15		
	16		
	17		
	18		
	19		
	20		
	21		
	22		
	23		
	24		
	25		
	26		
	27		
	28		
	29		
	30		
	31		
	32		
	33		
	34		
	35		
	36		
	37		
	38		
	39		
	40		
PLUS 7 PLAYS			**NEGATIVE PLAYS**

Figure 5-3. Sample offensive game opening script

RED ZONE OFFENSE		
LEFT HASH		RIGHT HASH
	PLUS 4 TO GOAL LINE	
	PLUS 10 TO PLUS 4	
	PLUS 25 TO PLUS 10	

TWO-POINT PLAYS		
LEFT HASH		RIGHT HASH
	FRONT & COVERAGE	

3RD DOWN		
LEFT HASH		RIGHT HASH
	1 - 3 YDS	
	4 - 6 YDS	
	7 - 10 YDS	
	EXTRA LONG	

4TH DOWN		
LEFT HASH		RIGHT HASH
	1 - 3 YDS	
	4 - 6 YDS	
	LONG	

COMING OUT		
LEFT HASH		RIGHT HASH
	NEG 1	
	NEG 3	
	3RD & 8+	
	3RD & 4-7	
	3RD & 1-3	

SPECIALS

VICTORY FOUR-MINUTE OFFENSE		
LEFT HASH		RIGHT HASH
	1	
	2	
	3	

Figure 5-4. Sample offensive game plan sheet by field zone and situation

Down	Run %	Pass %	Plays
1XL			
1L			
1M/1S			
2XL			
2L			
2M			
2S			
3L/3XL			
3M			
3S			
4L/4XL			
4M			
4S			

Blitzes	Opponent Formations – Top Plays

Figure 5-5. Sample defensive game plan sheet

SECTION 2

THE IN-SEASON: DON'T GET OVERWHELMED— STAY WITH YOUR PLAN

Many coaches coach only for the enjoyment of the game day. However, most experienced coaches, enjoy the entire year and all that goes into molding young people into a team. During the season, the clock seems to speed up. You never have enough hours in the day. You can never watch too much film, or go over the special play or adjustment too many times. If the coach is organized, and has planned ahead, the season will go much smoother. The job of the coach is more than just winning games. Keep perspective. Continue to be a shining light for your community and youth. Give back, and help other people have a great experience with your sport and your program.

6

Do for Others

Tip #22: At homecoming, invite your former players into the locker room for pre-game meetings and preparation.

Inviting former players into the locker room keeps the door open for former players to help you in your program. Former players become doctors, lawyers, construction workers, information technology professionals, and the list goes on. These men that played proudly for you will still want to feel like they are a part of the program, and they'll want to help where they can.

This practice is also a nice opportunity to give your current players an opportunity to see what they can become in a few short years, and how athletics helps shape a person for productive citizenship. Former players can make great role models. It's good for your current players to see your appreciation and consideration for your former players.

Tip #23: Develop a teacher-of-the-week award, and publicize it.

The teacher-of-the-week award can be done several ways. A good idea to help spread the honor around is to have each department be recognized each week. The players could vote on the teacher of the week from that department. It's a good idea to make a traveling plaque or trophy and certificates to give to each weekly winner that they can keep. Make sure to have your players make the presentation, so they get the practice of showing appreciation to other people that help them. In addition, make sure to take photos of the presentation to put in the school newspaper, team newsletter, or on the school (and/or team) website.

7

Continue to Provide a Framework for Success

Tip #24: Have a player-of-the-week program.

A player of the week can be done many ways. One of the priorities of a player-of-the-week program is to publicize the player and the program. Some football programs will award an offensive, defensive, special teams, and practice player for each week of the season. A good way to honor the players of the week is to buy them a special T-shirt and make or buy them a certificate. Make sure their teammates and coaches applaud the players of the week when you award them.

Tip #25: Have your players wear a special, players-only shirt on game days to school and to travel in.

Jerseys are to be worn on the field. Having your players wear a special polo-style shirt, crew-style shirt, or even a shirt and a tie is a good way to help the athletes develop an identity as a team. Athletes of today want to look like college or professional athletes. They will feel good wearing a shirt that is modeled after a shirt they could buy at the mall. Make sure the kids will want to wear the shirt. The emphasis of the shirt is to help improve the image of the team, as well as providing a unifying force for the team. The shirts can be purchased for each player, the players could buy their own, or the players could raise funds for the cost of the shirts.

Tip #26: Develop a team camp T-shirt that only players and coaches wear.

The team camp shirt could mention the theme for the season or display a graphic special to the team. If the graphic represents the theme for the season, it's a good idea to put the theme into code for the back of the shirt. Make sure the players can keep the themes to themselves and not share with non-team members. Make sure all players that attended camp and are participating have the opportunity to get a shirt. The shirt can be a unifying force.

The coaches or even the players can come up with the seasonal theme. The leadership council or captains could also have the bulk of the input on the theme as well as the T-shirt design. The camp T-shirt is a great idea to develop ownership in the program.

Tip #27: Have the players clean their own helmets, shoulder pads, and shoes.

By having players clean their own equipment, the coach is providing an opportunity for the athletes to be responsible. When a player cleans his own equipment, he is practicing the discipline of taking care of his own possession. This discipline is extremely valuable. In addition to cleaning the equipment, the players can also check for any snaps, buckles, straps, or strings that might need to be replaced.

Tip #28: Have your leaders develop a team warm-up CD for pregame warm-ups.

Allowing the athletes to have input in the songs they warm up to is a simple way of empowering your players. They will feel that they have a say in the program. The coach needs to double-check all songs for appropriateness.

This task is good for a leadership council, if you have one. The players on the leadership council are representatives of the team. Many teams have certain music they like to have played as they take the field, or as they warm up. Rather than doing this as a coach, it's a good idea to have the kids choose songs they want to hear and songs that will help them warm up more effectively. This approach provides another opportunity for kids to feel like they are special, as this is *their* warm-up music.

Tip #29: Create a weekly highlight video, and show it to your team the night before the next game.

Creating a weekly highlight video takes a few hours of time each week. The payoff is that the athletes will feel like they are each a big-time player when they see themselves in a highlight video. The highlight video can be made using basic video-editing software that comes standard on many computers. Additionally, the highlight video can be made using tendency software.

The highlight video should have some of the best plays from the previous week's game or practice, and the plays should be set to music. Many coaches also put motivational quotes or comments at the beginning or end of the video.

Highlight videos can be used for instruction as well as motivation. Many highlight videos are designed to set the stage for future success by getting players to believe that they can play perfectly and that they are a great team.

One way to manage the highlight video is to show the video to the team after practice, the day before the game. It can also be shown to the team on the day of the game, either in the morning before school or in the afternoon or evening during the pregame routine.

Tip #30: Watch the video with your players from your game within 24 hours of playing the game.

View the video with your players as soon after the contest as possible. This viewing needs to take place at a time when the game is still fresh in the minds of all participants. This screening is the best time to give accurate feedback to your players. Many football programs break their squads up by position groups to view the video with their position coaches.

Watching video from a game recently played helps players see what they've done right and wrong. Many times, if players can't see how they ran a play or missed a tackle or a block, they can't help but make the same mistake again. They say a picture is a worth a thousand words, and such is the case with video. To go along with the video analysis of a team, it's a good idea to grade each player on each play he participated in. This way, each player understands the importance of each play and the priority of playing each play as hard as they possibly can. Many times, the critique of the video will help learning occur much more efficiently.

Tip #31: Have Saturday morning breakfast with your players.

For teams that have games on Friday night, Saturday morning is a good time to watch film together. In addition to watching film, it's a good time to provide food for the kids, which will increase the attendance of the film session. For some athletes, it might be the only good meal they get for the weekend. This breakfast is also another time the players can be together, and another time the parents can be together while helping kids.

Just like with the pre-game meal, planning ahead and recruiting helpers is vital to success. Plan on spending 30 to 45 minutes eating together, and then viewing the film after that. Space will need to be requested ahead of time to serve and eat the food. Clean-up will also need to planned ahead for.

Tip #32: If you have the capability, put your game video or opponent video on your website for players to access.

Viewing video on the Internet is not a new concept, especially for today's athletes. Again, if you and your school have the capability, posting videos online is a great way for athletes to study film any time of day, not just before or after practice. Many football tendency software makers provide Internet capability with the software package.

The website will need to be password protected, so that only your players and coaches can watch the video. The video will have certain requirements to allow storage and viewing. The coach can also provide worksheets for players to fill out on the video they watch. The website will need to be updated at least one time per week, if not more.

Tip #33: Make copies of opponent video cut-ups for players to take home to watch.

If you can put your opponent's video on the Internet for player viewing, that is the most convenient way for the players to view video. If you cannot do this, then it will be important to make copies of the opponent's video cut-ups and distribute these cut-ups on DVDs to your players. The coach should provide a worksheet for players to fill out on the video assignment. Players can exchange DVDs with each other, based on what part of the game plan they are involved with.

Tip #34: Show your players' opponent video as much as possible.

Take every opportunity to allow your players to watch video of their next opponent. The players of tomorrow are more children of the Digital Age than ever before. They will learn more from viewing video than in the past. It's a good idea to watch video before and after practice, as well as whenever the athletes can fit it into their day.

Tip #35: Show video of practice to your players for improvement.

The season is a busy time with all the opponent video that the coaches and players need to watch to be prepared for the next game. With all the activities that go on during the season, keep in mind that teams spend the majority of their time on the practice field, practicing, and the minority of their time on the game field, playing the game. Some of the best teaching opportunities come from viewing video from practice.

Many times during practice, the starting team is running players versus a scout team. As the coach, you can show your players how the defense could adjust, you can show your players a better way to block a specific defensive front, or the coaching could be as simple as showing your player that his first step is three inches too long or short.

Tip #36: Develop a weekly scouting report to distribute to your players.

A scouting report is one of the best ways for your players to study opponent tendencies and the game plan. The scouting report is only as good as it is learned by the players that have to execute it on game day. A sample weekly scouting report is shown in Figures 7-1 through 7-3.

Opponent Punt

NHS uses a tight punt with the punter at 12 yards and the personal protector at 6 yards. The inside three will block down, the wing will fan, and the protector will fill.

They have a good get-off time of 1.81 seconds. They are not free releasers; they will protect a long time. The punter kicks the ball between 30 and 35 yards and can kick directionally. If it is fourth-and-short, they will try to draw you offside by popping up before they go into their stance.

Be prepared for spread punt as well.

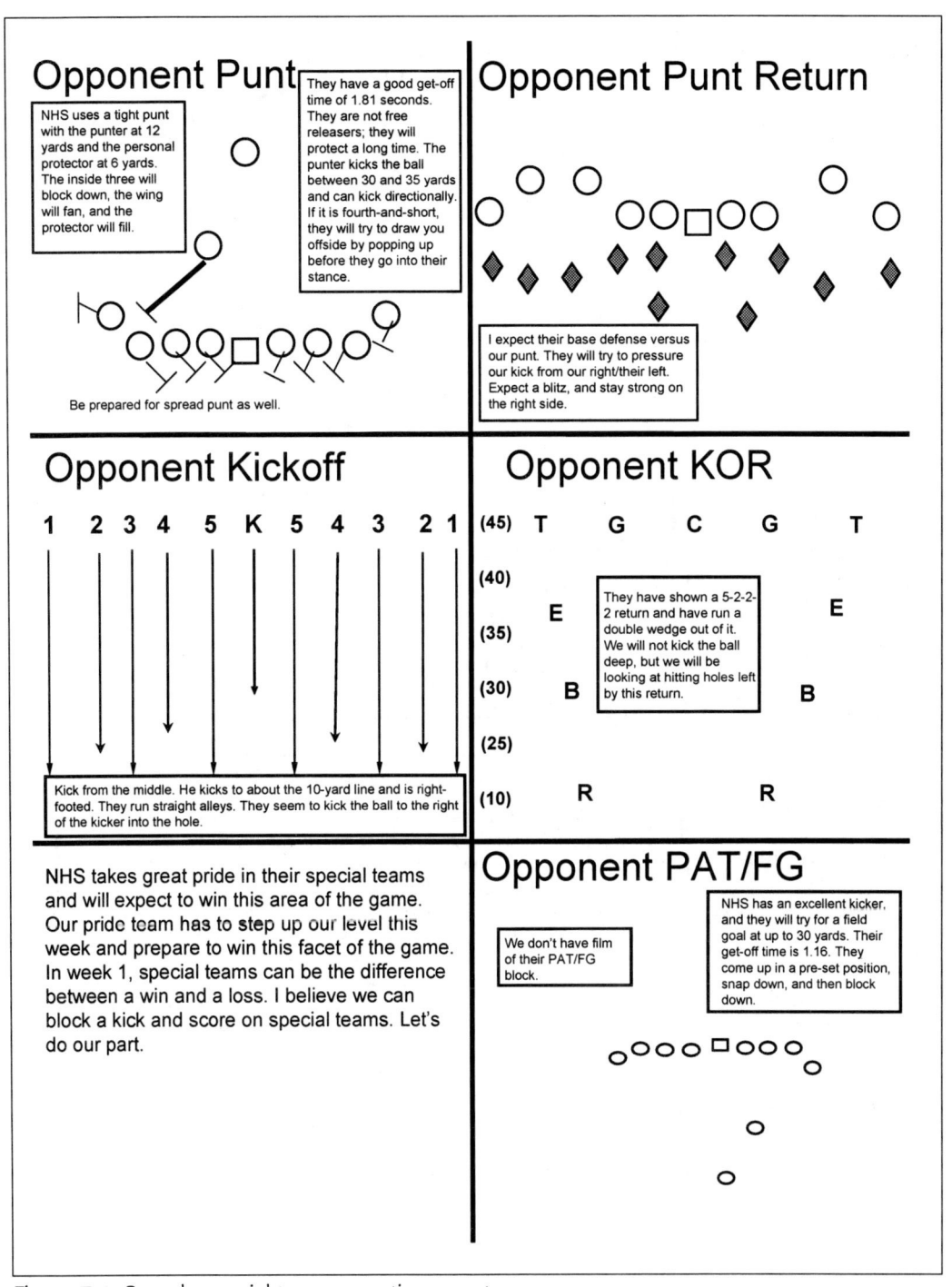

Opponent Punt Return

I expect their base defense versus our punt. They will try to pressure our kick from our right/their left. Expect a blitz, and stay strong on the right side.

Opponent Kickoff

1 2 3 4 5 K 5 4 3 2 1

Kick from the middle. He kicks to about the 10-yard line and is right-footed. They run straight alleys. They seem to kick the ball to the right of the kicker into the hole.

Opponent KOR

(45) T G C G T
(40)
(35)   E   E
(30)   B   B
(25)
(10)   R   R

They have shown a 5-2-2-2 return and have run a double wedge out of it. We will not kick the ball deep, but we will be looking at hitting holes left by this return.

NHS takes great pride in their special teams and will expect to win this area of the game. Our pride team has to step up our level this week and prepare to win this facet of the game. In week 1, special teams can be the difference between a win and a loss. I believe we can block a kick and score on special teams. Let's do our part.

Opponent PAT/FG

We don't have film of their PAT/FG block.

NHS has an excellent kicker, and they will try for a field goal at up to 30 yards. Their get-off time is 1.16. They come up in a pre-set position, snap down, and then block down.

Figure 7-1. Sample special teams scouting report

49

Opponent Offense

Multiple Pro

```
                    ⑤
                   ㊵
                    ④
      ⑧⑨ ㊲ ㊽ [55] ㊽ ㊽ ㊽        ①
         B   T  N  T        S
                                  C
            L   M   R
          C         F
```

#89	John Player	6'4"	215	11
#4	Bill Quarterback	5'9"	150	12
#44	Frank Fullback	5'8"	185	12
#5	Billy Fastback	5'8"	170	12
#1	John Receiver	6'2"	165	12
#86	Tight End	6'1"	215	12
#72	Jim Tackle	6'1"	305	12
#58	Jerry Guard	6'1"	255	12
#55	Jack Center	5'11"	215	12
#64	Steve Guard	6'3"	210	11
#75	Bob Tackle	6'4"	215	12

Subs:
#14 FL 5'10" 160 12
#15 QB 5'9" 150 11

Special

Points of Emphasis
DL: Pad level, feet, trigger, ball awareness
LB: Pad level, buzz steps, reads, pursuit
DB: Fits, pursuit, communication, stay on top
Defense: Pursuit and turnovers

Notes

NHS is a very good team. They see you as country kids who can't play at their level. They will look to come into your house and push you around. They are a multiple I team that will look to run the ball and throw play-action passes. Their offensive line has tight splits and will get off the ball. #5 is their best back; he has good speed and wiggle in the hips. We must swarm him and be strong tacklers. #44 is a hard-running fullback who will get the ball between 8 to 12 times a game, and he will try to run you over. #1 is their playmaker on the outside, and they will try and hit him deep. He is their fastest player. They have big tight ends and will probably use both a majority of the time. They love to throw to them on play-action and boot. They are in a QB quandary. I would expect to see two to three quarterbacks on Friday, all with different abilities. We need to jump on them early with our swarm, pursuit, and enthusiasm. We need to let the private rich kids know they can't come to the county and push us around.
Are you ready to gain the respect you deserve?

Figure 7-2. Sample defensive scouting report

Opponent Defense

4-2
Cover 3/1

#	Name	Height	Weight	Grade
#1	Ron Corner	6'2"	165	12
#5	Sam Safety	5'8"	170	12
#9	Steve Linebacker	6'2"	180	12
#14	Jim Corner	5'10"	170	12
#27	Will Linebacker	5'9"	180	12
#34	Sam Linebacker	6'0"	190	11
#43	John End	6'0"	210	12
#44	Mike Linebacker	5'8"	180	12
#55	Jack End	5'10"	195	12
#58	Jim Tackle	6'1"	230	12
#72	Bob Tackle	6'1"	305	12

Subs:
#75 DL 6'1" 200 11

Bear

4-1 / 4-3

3-2

Coverages:
1, 3, 2, Zero, 4

New:

Notes

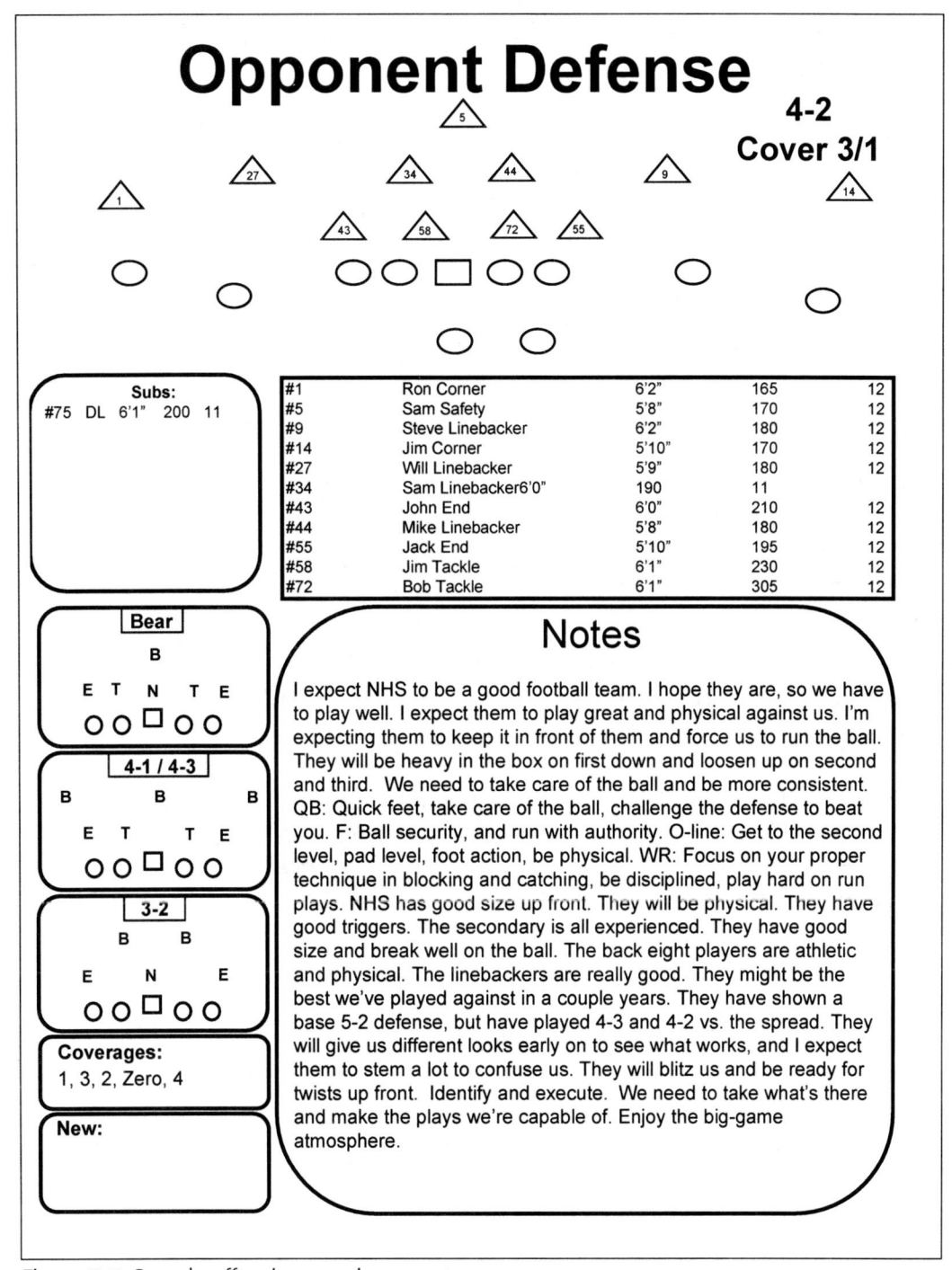

I expect NHS to be a good football team. I hope they are, so we have to play well. I expect them to play great and physical against us. I'm expecting them to keep it in front of them and force us to run the ball. They will be heavy in the box on first down and loosen up on second and third. We need to take care of the ball and be more consistent. QB: Quick feet, take care of the ball, challenge the defense to beat you. F: Ball security, and run with authority. O-line: Get to the second level, pad level, foot action, be physical. WR: Focus on your proper technique in blocking and catching, be disciplined, play hard on run plays. NHS has good size up front. They will be physical. They have good triggers. The secondary is all experienced. They have good size and break well on the ball. The back eight players are athletic and physical. The linebackers are really good. They might be the best we've played against in a couple years. They have shown a base 5-2 defense, but have played 4-3 and 4-2 vs. the spread. They will give us different looks early on to see what works, and I expect them to stem a lot to confuse us. They will blitz us and be ready for twists up front. Identify and execute. We need to take what's there and make the plays we're capable of. Enjoy the big-game atmosphere.

Figure 7-3. Sample offensive scouting report

Tip #37: Develop an itinerary for game day to distribute to your players.

The itinerary is a schedule for the game day. The itinerary will help all athletes be aware of where to be at specific times during the day and during the pregame routine. The itinerary can be used by the coach to list out the main points of the game plan on each side of the ball. It can also be used to communicate any last tips or pointers to the team. Additionally, the itinerary helps the head coach communicate with the assistant coaches with regard to times. A sample game-day itinerary is shown in Figure 7-4.

Tip #38: Have your players complete a quiz over the game plan on the day before your contest.

A quiz is a good idea to help cement the game plan into the minds of the athletes. The quiz could be done the day before the game or the day of the game. It's a good idea to include the main tendencies of the opponent, as well as any special or featured plays planned by your coaches. Figures 7-5 through 7-7 show examples of positional quizzes.

Tip #39: Use helmet awards to motivate your players.

Helmet awards can be a positive motivator if used the correct way. The best way to use helmet awards is award the stickers for achieving the win, and then award stickers to individual players for their contribution to achieving the group or position goals for the game. Keeping the awards team-, group-, or position-oriented helps to keep jealousy and negative feelings away from the helmet awards.

Many teams will create a team logo or use a school logo and have stickers made up to place on each player's helmet. One idea is to use the superman logo "S" in school colors and award the "S" to each player for each win of the season. Other "S" awards can be given out for reaching specific team or group goals set up before the season.

Players will take pride in having special award stickers on their helmets. They can place the award stickers anywhere they want on their helmets, and then when the season is over, they can take the award stickers with them. It's amazing how many 30- and 40-year-old men still treasure their helmet awards from high school. Presenting helmet awards is just another way for a high school player to feel valued as a part of the program.

Date:
Game #

8:00 a.m.	School starts; don't be late
2:55 p.m.	School is out; make wise choices
4:00 p.m.	Tapers report to locker room
4:25 p.m.	All players report to locker room
4:45 p.m.	Link up
4:55 p.m.	Quiet time, lights out
5:00 p.m.	Pre-game meetings (defensive position, offensive position, defense, pride offense)
5:35 p.m.	Team dynamic warm-up
5:45 p.m.	Kicking group out
6:00 p.m.	Passing group out
6:15 p.m.	Full dress
6:15 p.m.	Linemen gather under the goalpost
6:19 p.m.	Individual defense
6:22 p.m.	Individual offense
6:25 p.m.	Team defense
6:33 p.m.	Team offense
6:37 p.m.	War drill
6:42 p.m.	Locker room (captain's coin toss)
6:51 p.m.	Take the field for introductions
7:00 p.m.	Kickoff

Game Plan

Defense: Sprint to the ball, hit hard and take the ball away. Force at least three turnovers. Show great pursuit. Know your responsibilities and checks. Be great tacklers. Identify their formations and attack. Start each half fast. Be physical.

Offense: Execute, take what they give us and take care of the ball. Identify what they are giving us. Start each half fast.

Pride: Allow *no* big plays. Play smart. Block a kick; recover a kick. Win this phase.

Team: Compete, execute, and play hard. Play together at all times. Cheer for each other, and celebrate with each other. Be the more physical team. Play great!

"When you step on the field, you cannot concede a thing."
—Gayle Sayers

Figure 7-4. Sample game-day itinerary

Sample O-Line Quiz

Orange Hanes

```
   B    B    B
   T    N    T
 O  O  □  O  O
      O  O
```

Strawberry King 18

```
   B       B
   T    N  B  T
 O  O  □  O  O
      O  O
```

Grape Kilo 17

```
   B          B
   T    N  B  T
 O  O  □  O  O
      O  O
```

Blue Army

```
              B     B
    B    T  B  N    T
  O  O  O  □  O  O
         O  O
```

Pea Thong 51

```
     B    B
B    T    N  B  T  B
   O  O  □  O  O
         O  O
```

Brown Seminole 19

```
              B     B
       B    T  B  N   T  B
     O  O  □  O  O
            O  O
```

Broccoli Navy 16

```
              B    B
     B    T  B  N    T  B
        O  O  □  O  O
              O  O
```

Asparagus Jack 71

```
                    B
       B
       T  B  N  B  T  B
     O  O  □  O  O
           O  O
```

Figure 7-5. Sample offensive lineman quiz

Sample Skilled Player Quiz

Cat Stop	2 Bow	3 Left Gator
ooOoo	ooOoo	ooOoo
4 Right Option Right	3 Right Slide	4 Right Under
ooOoo	ooOoo	ooOoo
Cat Killer F Sweep Left	Cat Strong Drive	3 Left Slide Corner
ooOoo	ooOoo	ooOoo
3 Right Houston	Cat Vegas	4 Right Saddle
ooOoo	ooOoo	ooOoo
4 Left Sprint Left Smash	3 Left Strong Frisco	3 Left Chicago
ooOoo	ooOoo	ooOoo
2 Smoke	2 Split Special	3 Right Nasty Scat Crazy
ooOoo	ooOoo	ooOoo

Figure 7-6. Sample offensive skilled player quiz

Sample Defensive Quiz

Formations:
Spread	R-P	Plays:_____
Ace	R-P	Plays:_____
Trey	R-P	Plays:_____
Trips	R-P	Plays:_____
Gun Ace	R-P	Plays:_____
Gun Spread	R-P	Plays:_____

Down and Distance:

1XL	R-P	Plays:_____	3XL	R-P	Plays:_____
1L	R-P	Plays:_____	3L	R-P	Plays:_____
1M/1S	R-P	Plays:_____	3M	R-P	Plays:_____
2XL	R-P	Plays:_____	3S	R-P	Plays:_____
2L	R-P	Plays:_____	4XL/4L	R-P	Plays:_____
2M	R-P	Plays:_____	4M	R-P	Plays:_____
2S	R-P	Plays:_____	4S	R-P	Plays:_____

Stack Loop Check

Stack Loop Check

Stack Loop Check

Stack Loop Check

Stack Loop Check

Stack Loop Check

Figure 7-7. Sample defensive quiz

Tip #40: Take your team to a movie during the season.

Taking your team to a movie can help set the tone for a week, giving the kids an opportunity to not think about football, or just time to be with their teammates and friends. Make sure the movie is appropriate, have enough supervision, and don't be afraid to enlist the help of parents to help with transportation, snacks, or clean-up.

Going to a movie is just another opportunity for your team to bond. It's a time for kids to be kids, and they don't have to be worried about if they know who to block on the sweep or what the call is for running a reverse. It's great to do something non-sports-related during the season, just to take the pressure off of always having to be perfect. Many sports are so competitive, and many coaches who have to work hard at building a team are taking over programs that struggle with winning, so just trying to be competitive is a major goal of the program. It's difficult to maintain the interest of playing the sport and just having fun. Taking a team to a movie is a good release. It is also a great opportunity to let the kids know that you, as the coach, value them as more than just a player, but as a person as well.

Tip #41: Pray with your team.

Praying with your players can be a controversial subject in some areas of the country. Find out how your local school and community feel about prayer. If the opinion is against coach-led prayer, then ask some of your more mature, devout athletes to lead the team in prayer. Either way, one of the responsibilities of the coach is to provide leadership. The more positive examples of leadership you provide for your players, the better job you do. There is not a better example of leadership than Jesus Christ.

8

Ideas on How to Help Parents

Tip #42: Have your staff clean the varsity-level game uniforms.

Cleaning the game uniform is one of the most nerve-racking tasks a parent can undertake, when it comes to parental responsibilities, as a part of the team. Many parents are worried about cleaning the uniform and having it change colors during the process. Parents also struggle with getting the uniform cleaned in a timely fashion.

Cleaning the game uniform can help with public relations, by showing the parents that the coaches are willing to work for the kids outside of the coaching responsibilities. The parents will truly appreciate the work you put in, because it shows the parents you care about the presentation of their child.

Additionally, cleaning the uniforms as a staff makes sure the uniforms are cleaned consistently. Uniforms will be checked out on the day of the game and checked back in right after the game in the locker room. This process ensures that the uniforms are washed before any stains can set in. It also allows the coaches an opportunity to check the uniforms for rips or stains.

Tip #43: Provide a weekly study hall for athletes who are struggling academically.

Many athletes struggle with time management. Providing a study hall for those athletes can be just the little extra they need to stay eligible—or get recruited.

A typical schedule would be to provide a study hall before school two days a week for 30 to 45 minutes per session. Another option would be to provide the study hall after practice one day a week and on a Saturday morning for the other session. The study hall could be optional to all student-athletes and required for any student-athletes who currently have a D or an F in any subject. Coaches, older players needing volunteer hours, or even high school teachers who are willing to help could supervise the study hall. The extra time spent in study hall will make a difference for a large number of student-athletes, and it will also help support the parents of student-athletes by providing a structured environment to focus on academics.

Tip #44: Support your players' choices to achieve good grades.

Continually encourage your athletes to do their best in all areas of life. In addition, remind the athletes that they are at school for an education, not to find a mate or become an NFL star.

One way to help students with their academics is by having consequences for less-than-average grades. For example, restrict playing time for players who receive low grades during the week. Many schools have gradebooks that are posted on the school website. It is easy to check grades on a regular basis, and it's easy for students to see their progress of catching up if they fall behind. It's also a good idea to reward the student-athletes who do a good job in the classroom. Give an academic award each week and at the end of the season.

Tip #45: Have Thursday night meals for your team.

Thursday night meals, or the night-before-the-game meals, have become a ritual for many successful teams. Initially the Thursday night meal would appear to be a huge headache. The Thursday night meal can go just as smoothly as any other thing in your program that you plan ahead for.

It will be important to get donations ahead of time. Many businesses are proud to donate food to a school team. Donations allow the businesses to feel like they are a part of your success. Soliciting donations is a great project to delegate to the moms' squad. The moms can be divided into teams that each take a week and serve what they want, as long as the coach approves the menu ahead of time. Space will need to be reserved ahead of time. Procedures will need to be put into place with regard to who eats first, and who cleans up. The Thursday night meal has proven to be a good team-building time for players and parents as well. It can be the highlight of the week for many players.

Tip #46: Have a photographer available to take individual player action shots during games to sell to parents.

Having a photographer available is a win-win for your program. Parent and players get pictures from that special season to keep forever. The photographer has an opportunity to earn new business, and the athletic pictures can carry over to senior pictures, engagement and wedding pictures, as well as family pictures. One of the worst feelings in the world is to have a special event come up and think that the camera you are using will work just fine, and then getting the pictures back to find out the event has come and gone without one good, usable photograph. In addition to having the photographs for players and parents, the coach can negotiate to have copies of all pictures to use in newsletters or the website.

9

Connecting With the Community

Tip #47: Have an alumni game during the season.

An alumni game is a great way to involve the alumni. For football, this could be a flag football game or a fully padded game. Of course, when setting up a flag football game, it is much easier to organize and manage. Former players will not need to use any school equipment other than the flags. Conversely, if you organize a full-contact game, more former players might be interested in playing. The more former players who participate, the more people will come watch. If organizing an alumni padded football game, the coach has to be aware that the equipment will have to come from the program. So all players will have to check their equipment in, the alumni will have to check the equipment out, play the game and then check the equipment back in. The players will then have to recheck the equipment back out. In addition to giving the alumni the opportunity to come back and play on their former home game field, the alumni game is an opportunity to raise funds for your program.

Tip #48: Allow the youth teams to scrimmage at halftime during your home varsity contests.

With the help of the youth coaches, having a youth scrimmage at half time is a great way to include the young people in the program. The youth coaches will have to manage the scrimmage, as the entire varsity coaching staff will be making halftime adjustments in the locker room. This halftime scrimmage is a great experience for the youth to play under the lights in the stadium, like the big boys. The youth parents feel included, too.

The only possible negative would be if your field is not in good shape, then the extra playing on the field could be counterproductive to your program. If you play on a grass surface that is always in good shape, or if you play on artificial turf, this extra play will not be an issue.

To have this project work successfully, the coach will need to get administrative approval ahead of time, and then the coach will need to contact the game officials, so they know how long the halftime will be and what event is going on at halftime. The coach also needs to contact the opposing school, to let them know of the halftime schedule. Youth coaches will volunteer as halftime officials.

Tip #49: Encourage your youth teams to take the field with your varsity team.

Any time the high school coach can integrate the youth program into the high school program, it is beneficial. Taking the field on game night right before the opening kickoff is one of the most exciting things a junior high or senior high student can do. By allowing the youth teams to take the field with the high school team, it develops a sense of pride and excitement for the youth players.

It will be important to have proper supervision of the younger players, and safety is a priority. A good plan is to have the young players wait for the high school players at the edge of the field and as the older players pause and then take off onto the field, have the younger players follow behind the older players. This event will help the young players feel like they are part of the program. They will also feel like the cheers from the stands are for them as much as for the varsity team. Allowing younger team members to join the varsity when taking the field will also encourage the parents of the younger players to be at the game to see their child.

After the players take the field, the youth coaches or supervisors will then need to escort the young players off the field. You might take this opportunity to have the youth players all sit together in a special section.

Tip #50: For each home game, have an honorary captain at the coin toss.

The honorary captain for each home game could be the teacher of the week, a board member, or an administrator; a coach could even do a drawing for it and use it as a fundraiser. The honorary captain is another way to reach out to the community and include people from different backgrounds, while providing a positive experience.

It's important to have a schedule of the events that lead up to the coin toss, and make that schedule available to the honorary captain. It's also important to let the officials know before the coin flip that an honorary captain will be present at the coin flip. It's a good idea to publicize the honorary captain coin flip, and make sure the public address announcer has all the information necessary to make all the fans in attendance aware of the coin flip, and how to become an honorary captain.

It would be a good idea for the honorary captain to be able to wear a jersey or a team shirt to makes him feel special. Following the coin toss, it's a good idea to have the honorary captain escorted back to his seat.

Tip #51: Encourage the community to congratulate your players after their final home game of the season.

Many people of the community have watched your players grow up and remember them when they were knee high. The parents, players, and members of the community enjoy the opportunity to congratulate the players after their last home game. This receiving line is also a nice opportunity for elementary teachers to see their former students up close for the first time in years. It makes for an emotional event in a positive way.

A good procedure to follow is to have the public address announcer make an invitation during the second half of the game to all spectators to join the team after the game, at a specific location, to congratulate the team. This invitation could be followed up several times during the second half of the game. At the conclusion of the game, the coaches and players will stand in a single-file line at the specific location. A few spectators will need to know where to go and what to do. The coach can give the instructions to those few during the days leading up to the game. It is also appropriate for the coaches to lead the spectators through the line of players, congratulating each player along the way.

10

Evaluate and Prepare as a Staff

Tip #52: Video practice as regularly as possible.

Video is one of the best teaching tools you have at your disposal. Make sure, as the head coach, you provide video for your assistants to view. This viewing could be done on an individual basis, by the side of the ball, in football, or as an entire staff. It's a good idea to have the coaches take notes and then be ready to reteach the athletes from the notes.

When looking at the amount of time spent each week preparing for a contest versus the actual time spent in a contest, the ratio is almost five to one. It would make sense to record part of each practice during a week of preparation as well as the game itself. Players learn most by doing and watching themselves practice and then by doing again in the pursuit of perfection. A good plan of action is to record specific parts of practice, show the video to the players involved in that specific part of practice, and then give the players the opportunity to practice the same plays or routine as before. Videotape the second practice, and then allow the players a second time to evaluate their performance as they prepare to play in the game.

Additionally, recording drills in practice is a good way of keeping continuity in the program. New coaches and players can be taught from the video recording from the previous season.

Tip #53: Conduct a weekly self-scout of your program.

Developing a weekly self-scout is a good project for lower-level coaches, but no matter who does it, the self-scout is vital to your success. It's imperative that, as a coach, you know your tendencies. If you call for a wheel route on every second-and-long because it's your best second-and-long playcall, at least knowing that you make this call will help you be aware of other possible calls to make off of this tendency.

The same can be said for the defensive side of the ball. It's important to know when the defensive coaches are calling for blitzes and certain coverages. Just as you break down your opponents' tendencies, be sure they are breaking down your tendencies as well. You gain confidence in knowing what to expect.

Tip #54: Find former coaches or coaches of other sports to evaluate your program at practice.

Many times, as a coach, you sign an evaluation form after your season is completed, and if it was a good season with regard to wins and losses, you will see positive marks on the evaluation form. Conversely, if the season had too many losses and not enough wins, you will see more negative marks on the evaluation form. Administrators can't be at enough practices to truly evaluate what you do or how well you do it.

By developing a separate evaluation form, and having former coaches that had good levels of success, or successful coaches from other programs, evaluate your program, you can usually get better, more useable feedback to help you improve as a coach, a staff, and a program. Figure 10-1 shows a sample evaluation form.

iStockphoto/Thinkstock

[Name] High School Football Program Evaluation

Organization
1 2 3 4 5
Descriptors:
Field layout
On schedule/task
Smooth transitions

Professionalism
1 2 3 4 5
Descriptors:
Staff appearance
Interaction
Verbal

Enthusiasm
1 2 3 4 5
Descriptors:
Energy
Excitement
Voice and actions

Effort
1 2 3 4 5
Descriptors:
Coaches hustle
Players play hard

Leadership
1 2 3 4 5
Descriptors:
Consistently high standards
Commitment to excellence
Goal-oriented

Figure 10-1. Sample program evaluation form

Discipline
1 2 3 4 5
Descriptors:
Positive/firm
Constructive
Appropriate
Self

Attitude
1 2 3 4 5
Descriptors:
Positive
Team first
Respect others
Football important

Teaching
1 2 3 4 5
Descriptors:
Motivation
At player level
Effective techniques
Consistent feedback

Do the players respond to the coaches?	Yes	No
Do the coaches seek to connect with the players?	Yes	No
Is there an attitude of mutual respect?	Yes	No
Are these students having a positive experience?	Yes	No
Is the majority being taught to?	Yes	No
Is a commitment to excellence evident?	Yes	No
Would you want your child to be a part of this program?	Yes	No
Would you feel comfortable on this staff?	Yes	No

Evaluator _____ Date _____

Figure 10-1. Sample program evaluation form (cont.)

SECTION 3

THE POSTSEASON: FINISH STRONG—TIE UP ALL THE LOOSE ENDS

The postseason is very important to the continued success of your program. A well-organized postseason schedule will help any coach retain more athletes for the following year, promote graduating players, and help parents prepare for their children's college experience. Additionally, the postseason is a good time for reflection on how you did things in the previous season and how you can improve, while the season is still fresh in your mind.

11

Be Specific and Responsible

Tip #55: Develop an inventory of all the equipment you are responsible for.

It is important to develop an inventory of all your equipment. An inventory is helpful for insurance purposes. Every coach answers to someone with regard to finances and equipment. By developing an accurate inventory, you, as the coach, will show your respect for authority and your respect for the investment in your program. Most schools that hire a coach expect that coach to develop ownership for his program.

The inventory should list all equipment by type, the exact model, make, and manufacturer, as well as the condition of the individual piece of equipment. Microsoft Excel® is a good spreadsheet program to use to fill out your inventory. Another benefit to using a spreadsheet is, as the coach, you are showing your ability to use technology. A good time to do this inventory is immediately after your season. When checking in equipment, it is easier to count all uniforms, supplies, and equipment. Use assistant coaches to make the work go quicker. Again, if theft or accident occurs, and your equipment is stolen, damaged, or destroyed, having an up-to-date, specific inventory will help you replace your equipment. A sample inventory sheet is shown in Figure 11-1.

Item	Description		Quantity	Notes
Helmets	*Riddell*		78	
	VSR 4 Medium	12		
	VSR 4 Large	23		
	VSR 4 XL	2		
	Revolution M	7		
	Revolution L	22		
	Revolution XL	1		
	Schutt			
	Medium	7		
	Large	3		
	Adams	1		
Shoulder Pads	*Riddell*		95	We discarded 20 pairs that were old and in poor condition.
	Air Pac			
	Medium	45, 45, 45		
	Large	45 (7 pr), 55, 55, 57, 57, 18, 18, 44, 44, 77, 99		
	XL	68 (5 pr), 57 (3 pr), 45, 45, 55, 77		
	XXL	68 (3 pr), 99, 57		
	XXXL	68, 68		
	Evolution			
	Medium	18 (3 pr), 45 (4 pr), Ultra 45, 18 small		
	Large	Skill (4 pr), Line (1 pr)		
	XL	68 (4 pr), 45		
	XXL	68 ?		
	Power			
	Medium	86 DB (4 pr)		
	Large	96 QB (2pr), 56, 65, 96, 86 DB (6 pr), 19 DB flat, SPX 30, UP 1000		
	XL	96 (4 pr), 65, 19 DB (2), UP 1000, 86 DB (3 pr) 19 DB flat (3pr)		
	XXL	56, 19 DB flat, 86 DB		
	XXXL	86 ?		
	Rawlings			
	Medium	5 pr		
	Large	10 pr		
	XL	1, 2 pr belted		
	ATI	1 L		
	Adams	1 pr large		

Figure 11-1. Sample inventory sheet

Tip #56: Develop a budget.

Whether a budget is your responsibility or not, it is a good idea to know how much money you are asking for each year, and how much you are spending. Developing a budget goes back to the respect and the ownership issues. It is a good idea to do some research on other programs that are similar to yours. Some schools will spend more money if they know that they are handicapping their own coaches by underspending. When doing research, make sure to identify successful programs.

A budget or budget request is another good piece of information to enter into a spreadsheet. A sample list of budget requests and estimated dollar amounts is shown in Figure 11-2.

Player Equipment		
Quantity	Item	Cost
150	Mouthpieces (red)	
20	Travel bags	$11.00 per
8	Belted shoulder pads	$1,000.00 Riddell *got 8 pr
12	Revolution helmets	$1500.00-1800.00 *
2	Neck restrictors	$40.00 per Mueller collar-black cloth "cool one"
6	Home game pants (Riddell: 1 L, 3 XL, 2 XXL)	
6	Away game pants (Riddell: 1L, 3 XL, 2 XXL)	
60	Red game belts, cloth-covered	$4.00 per Riddell
	Hemet decals	$600.00, I'll order
	Award decals	$400.00, I'll order
12	Player game towels	$4.00 per - $48.00 white Wilson/ Velcro
500-600	Screw-in cleats	$50.00 1/2-inch metal tipped
10	Kneepads (pairs)	$50.00, Schutt DKP-VA dipped
2	Spider underpad	$30.00
100	Links	$80.00 Amsterdam printing #1 printed w/ "[Name] Football," I'll order
100	Shallow T nuts for helmets	$22.00
100	Normal depth T nuts	
50	Poly washers	
50	Stainless washers	
1	Totally tee	$12.00
	Reconditioning	$2,700.00

Figure 11-2. Sample budget request sheet

Tip #57: Keep accurate statistics and records.

Find a way to track the statistics of your players. Based on experience, it has almost always been better to recruit parents or teachers to help take statistics during the game, rather than try to record statistics from film the day after the game. Many times, these people are proud of what they do for the kids in your program. As long as they are appreciated, it will be easy to get volunteers.

In addition to recording and tracking statistics, it is important to provide these statistics to any media outlets in your area. Published statistics amount to free advertising for your program and for the talents of your players. By reporting statistics to media outlets, you are doing a major favor for yourself when it comes to parent relations. Statistics and records tracking goes a long way to proving your interest in your players and their possible recruitment, especially in the eyes of their parents. A sample form for statistics is shown in Figure 11-3.

Offense	Catches	Yards	Rushes	Yards	TDs	PATs	Passes	Comp	Yards	Points	Tot. Yds
Aaron King	69	1,570	7	57	27	3				168	1,627
Adam Amato	5	62	112	787	6	1				38	849
Van Ellis	58	860	41	528	17	1	1	0	0	104	1,388
Josh Gregory	3	28	4	5							33
Jordan Webb *65.4%			67	247	5	4	280	183	3,159	38	3,406
Chris Sperry	29	387			7	2				46	387
Patrick Carey	19	211	2	-7	3		1	0	0	18	204
Roy Davis			31	516	9					54	516
Jed Neider	2	32	0	0	4					24	32
Malcolm Stanley			11	29		1	3	2	31	2	60
Rob Baser			15	86	2					12	86
Mike Fennell	1	21									21

Jordan Webb 47 td passes with 5 int

Defense	Tackles	Assists	TFL	F. Rec.	Int.	Sacks		Tackles
Tony Crews	68	14	7	1	1	5	Eric Gaither	1
Jed Neider	60	18	13	1	1	8	Patrick Gerrein	1
Jared Bay	32	11	3	1		3	Nathan Hoeft	5
Rob Baser	22	3	2	1	1	1	Patrick Carey	3
Nathan Martin	28	13	2			1	Jonathan Mitchell	2
Steve Schaefer	36	10	2			3	Bobby Bridges	2
Nate Brack	23	4				1	Colter Janssen	1
Roy Davis	59	8	9	2		7	Donnie Abbott	1
Josh Gregory	41	10					Adam Amato	1
Darron Bardot	25	4	2	2	1	1	Cory Birkmann	1
Van Ellis	33	6			1		Mike Vemmer	1
Andrew Leicht	10	2				2	Andrew Bromet	1
Aaron King	11	1			3			
Malcolm Stanley	18	5			3			
Mike Fennell	9	1						
Jarred Cahill	8	4				1		
Corey Bailey	1	1						
Brad Bromet	4	1						
Adam Unnerstall	4	1						
David Kolb	8	2				1		
James Barnhart	3							

Special Teams	Punts	Avg.	KOR	Avg.	PRT	Avg.	Blocks	
Jordan Webb	13	35.6						
Van Ellis			9	26.1	16	11.4		
Aaron King			4	9.75			1	
Rob Baser							2	
Roy Davis			1	22			2	
Jed Neider							2	
Josh Gregory							1	

Figure 11-3. Sample statistics form

Tip #58: Keep game, season, and career records for your program.

Keeping track of these school records and posting them give the records more credibility. Athletes take pride in seeing their name up on the wall. Your program will have the appearance of a more established program by posting individual and team records.

These records can also be posted on the school website, and they can be published in a school newsletter. These records are best updated immediately following your season. A sample list of records is shown in Figure 11-4.

Another good way to build on the idea of tradition is to keep track of and post the program year-by-year won-lost records. Athletes can then see which years were the most successful in the history of the program, giving them a specific target to shoot for when trying to be the most successful team in school history or match a win total. Displaying the program's history also helps tie in current athletes and teams with athletes and teams from the past. In addition, making players aware of the program's past success can help develop the identity of a positive tradition. A sample year-by-year won-lost list is shown in Figure 11-5.

Team Records

Most points one season	Most yards gained rushing one game
Least points allowed one season	Most yards gained passing one game
Most yards gained rushing one season	Most total yards gained one game
Most yards gained passing one season	Least yards allowed one game
Most total yards gained one season	Least yards allowed rushing one game
Most interceptions one season	Least yards allowed passing one game

Individual Records

Most points scored one season	Most pass receptions career
Most points scored career	Most yards gained receiving one game
Most extra points scored one season	Most yards gained receiving one season
Most extra points scored career	Most yards gained receiving career
Most touchdowns scored one season	Most touchdowns passing one game
Most touchdowns scored career	Most touchdowns passing one season
Most yards gained rushing one game	Most touchdowns passing career
Most yards gained rushing one season	Most tackles one game
Most yards gained rushing career	Most tackles one season
Most yards gained passing one game	Most tackles career
Most yards gained passing one season	Most interceptions one season
Most yards gained passing career	Most interceptions career
Most passes completed one game	Longest interception return
Most passes completed one season	Longest punt return
Most passes completed career	Longest kickoff return
Most pass receptions one game	Longest run from scrimmage
Most pass receptions one season	Longest field goal

Figure 11-4. Sample records list

History of Union Wildcat Football

Year	Record	Conf. Finish	State Playoff	Coach
1965	Played Junior Varsity Schedule			Campbell
1966	3-6			3-6 33.3% 1966
1967	4-5			Chris Straub
1968	6-2-1			17-9-1 62.9% '67-'69
1969	7-2	2nd		
1970	5-4	2nd		Del Rinne
1971	6-2-1	2nd		185-89-1 67.3% '70-'95
1972	7-2	CO-Champs		275 games
1973	6-3	3rd		26 seasons
1974	6-3	2ND		
1975	10-1	Championship	Semi-Finals	
1976	6-3	CO-Champs		
1977	5-4	2nd		
1978	5-5	2nd		
1979	6-4	3rd		
1980	10-3	Co-Champs	Semi-Finals	
1981	6-4	2nd		
1982	11-2	CO-Champs	Semi-Finals	
1983	11-3	CO-Champs	Show-Me Bowl 2nd	
1984	8-3	Championship	District	
1985	9-2	Championship	District	
1986	8-3	2nd	District	
1987	6-4	4th		
1988	6-6	4th	Sectionals	
1989	10-1	Championship	Sectionals	
1990	11-1	Championship	Quarterfinals	
1991	10-2	Championship	Quarterfinals	
1992	6-5	CO-Champs	District	
1993	3-7			
1994	2-8			
1995	6-4			
1996	2-8			Tom Rahl
1997	7-3	3rd		20-30 40% '96-'00
1998	5-5	4th		
1999	3-7			
2000	3-7			
2001	3-7			Mike Hunter
2002	6-4			14-17 45% '01-'03
2003	5-6		District	
2004	2-8			Rex Grimes 2-8 20% 2004
2005	4-6	3rd		Brent Eckley
2006	10-1	Championship	District	51-17 75% 2005-present
2007	9-2	2nd	District	
2008	11-1	Championship	Sectionals	
2009	6-5	2nd	District	
2010	11-2	Championship	Quarterfinals	

All-time Record: 298-176-2   62.6%   476 total games   45 seasons   34 winning seasons

Figure 11-5. Sample year-by-year won-lost record list

Tip #59: Submit state record-holders to your state association.

If you are fortunate enough to coach in a state that has a sports record book, take the time to research the records, and submit any record-breaking events by your players or team. This information is another good way to advertise your program; it also builds your image with your parents. The parents will take pride in any records your team achieves, especially when their child is a part of the record-breaking performance.

Contact your state athletics association to determine if the state tracks records. If they do, request a record nomination form. Fill out the form, get validated by a supervisor/administrator, and send the nomination form to the state association.

12

Pay Your Players Back

Tip #60: Encourage your players to try other sports.

Almost all schools have the need to share their best athletes. An athlete participating in two or more sports happens at the college level, and these days even professional athletes participate in more than one sport. You may not have a Bo Jackson or a Deion Sanders, but you need to encourage kids to try more than the sport that you coach. It's in the student's best interest, and sooner or later the student will appreciate the coach who makes an effort to help the student without specifically helping themselves. In addition to helping the student gain a better educational experience, encouraging your athletes to participate in other sports gives them the opportunity to be exposed to more competition. Many times, the more talented teams don't beat the lesser talented teams because the lesser talented teams have more athletes who refuse to lose. They have that competitive spirit. The competitive spirit is developed by exposure to competition. Finally, the athlete who leaves your program and participates on another team can work as a recruiter for you on his new team.

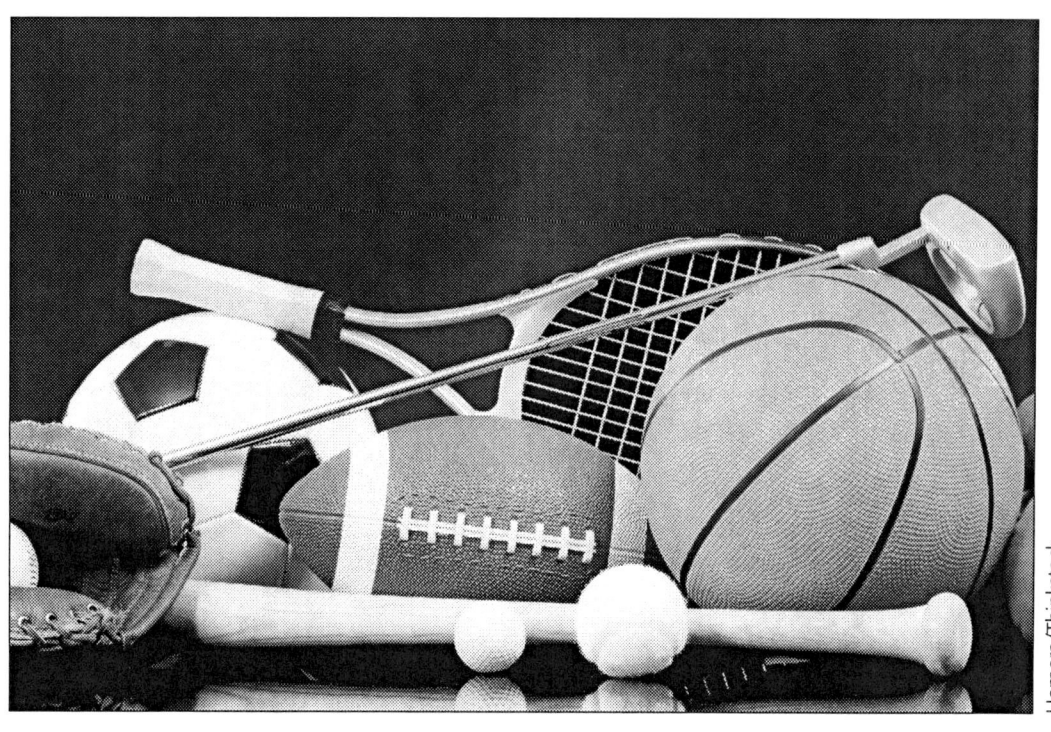

Tip #61: Celebrate a special season by having each member of the team sign a game ball to be displayed in the school trophy case.

Having a signed ball is a great way to commemorate conference or district championships, state playoff appearances, or undefeated seasons, and build pride in your program. Every time a player walks past the trophy case, he will walk a little taller, knowing he was part of something special that the entire school is proud of. This gesture is also another way to promote your successful program.

It's easy to use one of your game balls or to order a special autograph ball for players to sign. Have the players sign it at the end-of-the-season banquet. Make sure to get permission from your administration before starting this process.

Tip #62: Develop an end-of-the-season book.

Creating an end-of-the-season book is a great way to thank your players. The book is not an overwhelming task if the press clippings are saved in a way that can be mass-produced. Sections of media guides, individual, group, class, and team pictures can be used. Additional material can be pulled from newspapers, the Internet, and even scouting reports. It's also good to include final season statistics and any honored performers. It is good to collect anything that has been publicized about your team to put into the book.

An end-of-the-season book is a good project to delegate to a lower level coach or even a parent. Make sure the responsible person has access to all media outlets. The end-of-the-season book is a scrapbook for each of your players. The end-of-the-season book could be given out at the end-of-the-season banquet. The books make for a great parting gift from the program to the athlete. The books can be bound at an affordable price.

Tip #63: Develop a seasonal highlight video.

A highlight video is another great gift. However, many programs use highlight videos as a fundraiser. Many parents are willing to purchase highlight videos of their child's senior season. Larger programs on big budgets outsource the production of their highlight video. A reason for making your own program's highlight video is you maintain a personal touch with the athletes. Developing the ability to make a highlight video is also a good marketable skill if you find yourself looking for a job.

The process of making the video involves taking the video footage from all the games of the season (and all video angles shot) and entering them into a video-editing system on a computer. The video will then need to be sorted file by file, and discard the non-highlight video clips. The video will then need to be synchronized for different video angles. Transitions and titles will need to be added to the video, and then music will need to be added. The entire project will need to be rendered, checked for errors, and then finally copied to a DVD. After the DVD is created, it can be mass copied. Some programs will also create custom DVD labels, commemorating the season. A sample highlight order form is shown in Figure 12-1.

Highlight Order Form

2011 Highlight Video	$15.00	_____
2011 Season Individual Game Videos	$10.00 each game	_____
2010 Highlight Video	$15.00	_____
2010 Season Individual Game Videos	$10.00 each game	_____
	Total	_____

Name _____

Address _____

Phone _____

Email _____

Amount enclosed _____

Make checks out to John Coach.

Figure 12-1. Sample highlight order form

Tip #64: Develop a postseason routine for college-bound athletes.

One of the most important decisions in the life of a person is their college choice. It is imperative that, as the coach, you do everything in your power to promote the athletes from your program. Many coaches develop a presentation for each senior athlete that can be viewed by college coaches. When developing a presentation, include the athlete's name, height, weight, grade-point average, core grade-point average, class rank, ACT/SAT score, address, email, phone number, cell phone number, and parents' name(s). In addition, statistics and athletic as well as academic honors should be included. A sample senior presentation form is shown in Figure 12-2.

In addition to sending out information, it is important to make good quality video available to recruiters. As the coach, you can have your players develop their own highlight video, or some video editing software programs have features that allow for you to make a highlight tag with the player's number, and then at the end of the season, you can pull up all the video clips that are tagged with the player's individual number. If it is not possible to create an individual highlight video, then you can send a team highlight video and add in the particular player's best two games.

As a coach, it's important to find out the best way to market your graduating athletes. This approach might be just being available when college coaches come through your school. You, as the coach, might have to call the schools that interest your players. Make sure to fill out and return every questionnaire that is sent to you. Don't shortchange your players who have been committed to your program for several years.

Organization is the main priority when executing the postseason routine. All of the legwork needs to be completed within three to four weeks of the completion of your season. One other note: students will need to fill out a form that gives permission to release information. It's a good idea to have this done before the senior season, so have all players fill out the form at the conclusion of the season, and get parent signatures as well. Keep these forms on file.

NAME	NO.	HT	WT	SCHOOL	POSITION	STATS	CONTACT INFO	GPA	ACT
John Receiver	10	6'0	175		WR/DB/Returner	Offense: 67 catches for 1,034 yds, 9 TDs; Defense: 76 tackles, 1 sack, 2 fbl rec, 4 int	address, phone number, cell number, email	2.5	22
Bill Lineman	78	6'2	240		OL	2-yr starter, 1st team all-conf (2009, 2010), all-dist, all-area oline (2009)	address, phone number, cell number, email	3.25	27
Steve Linebacker	6	5'7	165		LB	72 tackles, 23 assists, 8 sacks, 2 fbl rec, 3 int, 2nd team all-conf (2009, 2010)	address, phone number, cell number, email	3.79	28
Jim End	4	6'0	180		DE	39 tackles, 14 assists, 1st team all-conf (2010)	address, phone number, cell number, email	2.37	29

Figure 12-2. Sample senior presentation form

Tip #65: Meet with each player individually.

The individual postseason meeting serves two purposes. The first purpose is to reflect and evaluate with each of your players. The immediate postseason is a great time to get feedback on everything in your program (e.g., favorite drills, practice length, the summer weight-training schedule, favorite coach). It is a good idea to have a form for the players to fill out. Ask what you want to find out about. Make sure the players know the meetings and forms are confidential. A sample postseason player evaluation form is shown in Figure 12-3.

The second purpose of the postseason meeting is to set the stage and plan for the future. For returning players, you can share your expectations and aspirations for the next season. This meeting is also a great time to find out from returning player how good they think the next team will be. This meeting is a good way to develop confidence in your next team. For the graduating players, the postseason is a great time to help guide them in the major decisions that are quickly approaching. Gather information, and offer to help. Follow through with your offers. A sample postseason player questionnaire is shown in Figure 12-4.

Head Coach Evaluation Form

Athletes' comments about a head coach are an important part of our staff evaluation process. Your thoughtful, constructive responses will help to improve our sports program. These comments are strictly confidential.

Grade: 9   10   11   12

Your role for the majority of the season: (check one)
- ❑ Started more than half of the contests
- ❑ Played regularly but started less than half of the contests
- ❑ Played in less than half of the contests
- ❑ Practiced only

Overall, I rate my coach:

1	2	3	4	5
Poor	Needs Improvement	Satisfactory	Very Good	Excellent

My coach's greatest strengths are:

Note any areas of concern or additional comments regarding your coach:

My coach is knowledgeable of sport techniques:

1	2	3	4	5
Strongly Disagree	Disagree	Neutral	Agree	Strongly Agree

My coach's greatest strengths regarding sport techniques are:

I respect my coach:

1	2	3	4	5
Strongly Disagree	Disagree	Neutral	Agree	Strongly Agree

I respect my coach most for:

My coaches clearly explain my role in contributing to the overall team's performance:

1	2	3	4	5
Strongly Disagree	Disagree	Neutral	Agree	Strongly Agree

My head coach is committed to my academic progress:

1	2	3	4	5
Strongly Disagree	Disagree	Neutral	Agree	Strongly Agree

My head coach is willing to make accommodations for classes:

1	2	3	4	5
Strongly Disagree	Disagree	Neutral	Agree	Strongly Agree

My head coach prepares me for each contest motivationally, strategically, and physically:

1	2	3	4	5
Strongly Disagree	Disagree	Neutral	Agree	Strongly Agree

My head coach treats me with respect:

1	2	3	4	5
Strongly Disagree	Disagree	Neutral	Agree	Strongly Agree

Any other comments (fairness, organization, other):

Figure 12-3. Sample postseason player evaluation form

How well do you think we did this last year? How close to our potential did we play? How close to your potential did you play?

What did we do well? What could have we done better? How?

What was your favorite drill? What was your least favorite drill?

What was the best part of practice? Worst?

Who were our best leaders last year?

What would you change about our program (our coaching staff, schedule, practice)? How? Why?

What is the best thing about our football program?

Underclassmen: What do you need to improve on for next year? How will you do it? What personal goals do you have for next year?

Will you play football next year? If so, what positions do you want to play? If not, why?

How good can we be next year? Better/worse? How many wins? Why?

Who should play next year that didn't this year? How will you convince those people to play?

Was the summer program and camps a worthwhile investment of time?

Figure 12-4. Sample postseason player questionnaire

13

Celebrate and Schedule With Parents

Tip #66: Create a yearly calendar, and distribute it to parents.

Giving a calendar to your parents in a timely fashion could be one of the best public relations moves you can make as a coach. By giving the parents a calendar, you are letting them know that you are planning for the future. You are showing the parents the priorities of your program. More importantly, you are giving the parents an opportunity to plan vacations, appointments, and all the other things that go on in their lives. Parents appreciate this.

This calendar could be a Word® document or listed in a spreadsheet, whichever format that, when presented, looks more organized. Date the calendar, and put the word "tentative" (or "TBD") on the calendar so that when you have to update the schedule, you can make the needed changes and redistribute a new dated calendar. A sample yearly calendar is shown in Figure 13-1.

Hemera/Thinkstock

[Name] High School Football Calendar 20XX
5/23/XX (Tentative)

December	Off-season—Phase I
January 3–March 21	Off-season—Phase II
March 24–May 16	Off-season—Phase III
March 18–May 15	Open gyms Tuesday/Thursday mornings 6:30–6:50 a.m.
April 15	Parent meeting on recruitment 6:00 p.m. FAC
April 9–May 21	Open field Wednesdays 5:30–7:00 p.m.
June 2–July 23	Summer school weight training (see calendar for times)
May 28	7-on-7 3:00 p.m. practice field
June 4–July 23	Open field 10:00-11:30 a.m. (Wednesdays only)
June 8–12	High school team camp 4:00–8:30 p.m.
June 13–14	Team camp 12:00–8:00 p.m.
June 5	7-on-7 passing league 5:00 p.m.@ TBD
June 19	7-on-7 passing league 6:00 p.m.@ TBD
June 26	7-on-7 passing league 6:00 p.m.@ TBD
June 27–28	Family float
July 10	7-on-7 passing league 6:00 p.m.@ TBD
July 11	Moms football clinic 6:00 p.m.
July 13–17	High school team camp 4:00–8:30 p.m.
July 23	Last day of summer school weight training
July 24–August 10	Vacation
August 7–8	Coaches' meetings (Time TBD)
August 11	First official practice 3:00–8:30 p.m.
August 14	First day in full pads 3:00–8:30 p.m.
August 15	Media day: HS: 3:00 p.m.
	Practice 4:30–7:00 p.m.
	Lock-in 9:00 p.m.–8:00 a.m.
August 16	Scrimmage 8:30–11:30 a.m.
	Parent meeting/family meal 12:00–1:30 p.m.
	Booster Club meeting/meal 6:00 p.m.
August 22	Jamboree @ FHS 6:00 p.m.
August 29	First game @ RHS
September 1	Labor Day: We will practice 3:00–6:30 p.m.
October 30 generally	Thursday game 10 vs. SHS; we will practice each day after this date, in the afternoon.
November 5	First-round playoff game
November 10	Second-round playoff game
November 15	Third-round playoff game
November 22	Fourth-round playoff game
November 29	State championship game

Figure 13-1. Sample yearly calendar

Tip #67: Develop an end-of-the-season banquet and program.

An end-of-the-season banquet is an opportunity to brag on your players and in turn give the parents an opportunity to be proud of their child and the job they've done as a parent. Some coaches use a PowerPoint® presentation, some coaches use a slide show or a video, and other coaches do a traditional program. It is good to give individual awards, especially if the team members vote on them. A sample of a team ballot is shown in Figure 13-2. This banquet is an opportunity to share positive stories about each player. If time doesn't allow, a coach could share about each senior. Any honors or awards should be presented at the program. The banquet is also a good opportunity to brag on your program, especially if you had any records broken during the season.

The banquet or program is a good opportunity to thank parents. The child or anyone else won't typically thank the parents. In addition to thanking parents, this event is a good time to thank your assistant coaches, filmers, statisticians, gate workers, press, administration, and anyone else who has helped make the season run smoothly. Following is a sample of a postseason banquet agenda:

- Announcements
- Introduce coaches
- Thank-yous
    - ✓ Filmers
    - ✓ Stats
    - ✓ Thursday-night meals
    - ✓ Saturday-morning meals
    - ✓ Ball boys
    - ✓ Managers
- Letterman
- Player voted awards
- Postseason awards
- Off-season challenge
- Dismiss

Team Ballot

Captains	1 _____
	2 _____
	3 _____
	4 _____
MVP	1 _____
Most Improved	1 _____
Most Dedicated	1 _____
	2 _____
MV Skilled Player	1 _____
MV Lineman	1 _____
MV Offensive Player	1 _____
MV Defensive Player	1 _____
Hardest Hitter	1 _____
Funniest Teammate	1 _____
Toughman Award	1 _____
MV JV Player	1 _____
MV Freshman	1 _____
	2 _____

Figure 13-2. Sample team ballot

14

Reflect and Evaluate

Tip #68: Go watch other successful teams practice.

Watching successful teams practice is a great opportunity to see how other people manage practice and how they run their program. If your season is finished, but the playoffs are going on, try to watch a team from another classification practice. Find successful programs to try to get new ways to improve. The immediate postseason is a great time of the year to view another program as they practice in the postseason. Watching another team practice might give you new ideas on how to manage a postseason practice.

Tip #69: Meet with each of your coaches.

The immediate postseason is the time to find out what staff changes will need to be made for the following season. As you meet with each assistant coach individually, be prepared and have an evaluative instrument or form for the coach to fill out. Immediately following the season is an important time to get feedback from your assistants while the drills, routines, and procedures are still easily remembered. Your program can grow if you can get open, honest feedback from your assistant coaches. Have your coaches evaluate themselves, their fellow coaches, and the head coach. A sample evaluation form is shown in Figure 14-1. Ask the assistant coaches to evaluate the off-season, the practice schedules, the game plan organization, and anything else that you think you can improve in the program.

Coaches Evaluation

What was your number-one contribution to our football program this year?

What duties and responsibilities off the field do you feel best about? What needs to be improved?

What is the best thing we did as a coaching staff?

What is the one thing that we, as a staff, need to do better?

On my side of the ball, the best thing we did was:

On my side of the ball, the one thing we should focus on to improve is:

The thing I'm most determined to improve for next year in my coaching is:

The thing I'm most proud of in my coaching this year is:

On a scale of 1 to 10, being the best, evaluate yourself in the following areas:

I get along with coaches, teachers, and administrators.	_____
My players perform great. They play the way I coach them to play.	_____
I have a good knowledge of our offensive/defensive scheme.	_____
I did a great job of performing my non-football duties	_____
I am loyal to the program and to the head coach.	_____
My kicking game responsibility performed well.	_____
I motivated my players to play to the best of their ability every game.	_____
I treated starters and non-starters with the same concern and respect, on and off the field.	_____
I worked my position players as hard as possible on a consistent basis.	_____
My position players respect my coaching ability and knowledge of the game. They have no doubt that I care for them off the field as much as on.	_____
I was always well-prepared for practice and player meetings.	_____

Figure 14-1. Sample evaluation form

I did a great job of communicating to my players exactly where they
stood on the depth chart and why.   _____

I do a good job of evaluating my position players, and I am objective in my
evaluation of their performance.   _____

Do you believe that off-the-field duties were split up in an equitable manner?

What areas can we improve in the kicking game?

Was our weekly practice schedule as efficient as it could be? Do you have suggestions as to how we might improve our weekly and daily practice schedules?

As a defense, what is the one thing we did best?

What is the most important thing we need to improve for next year?

Are there any ways in which you would like to change or alter our practice or meeting routine?

Do a depth chart of all underclassmen offensive and defensive linemen.

How can we improve our Saturday and Sunday preparation?

As an offense, what is the one thing we did best?

On special teams, what is the one thing we did best?

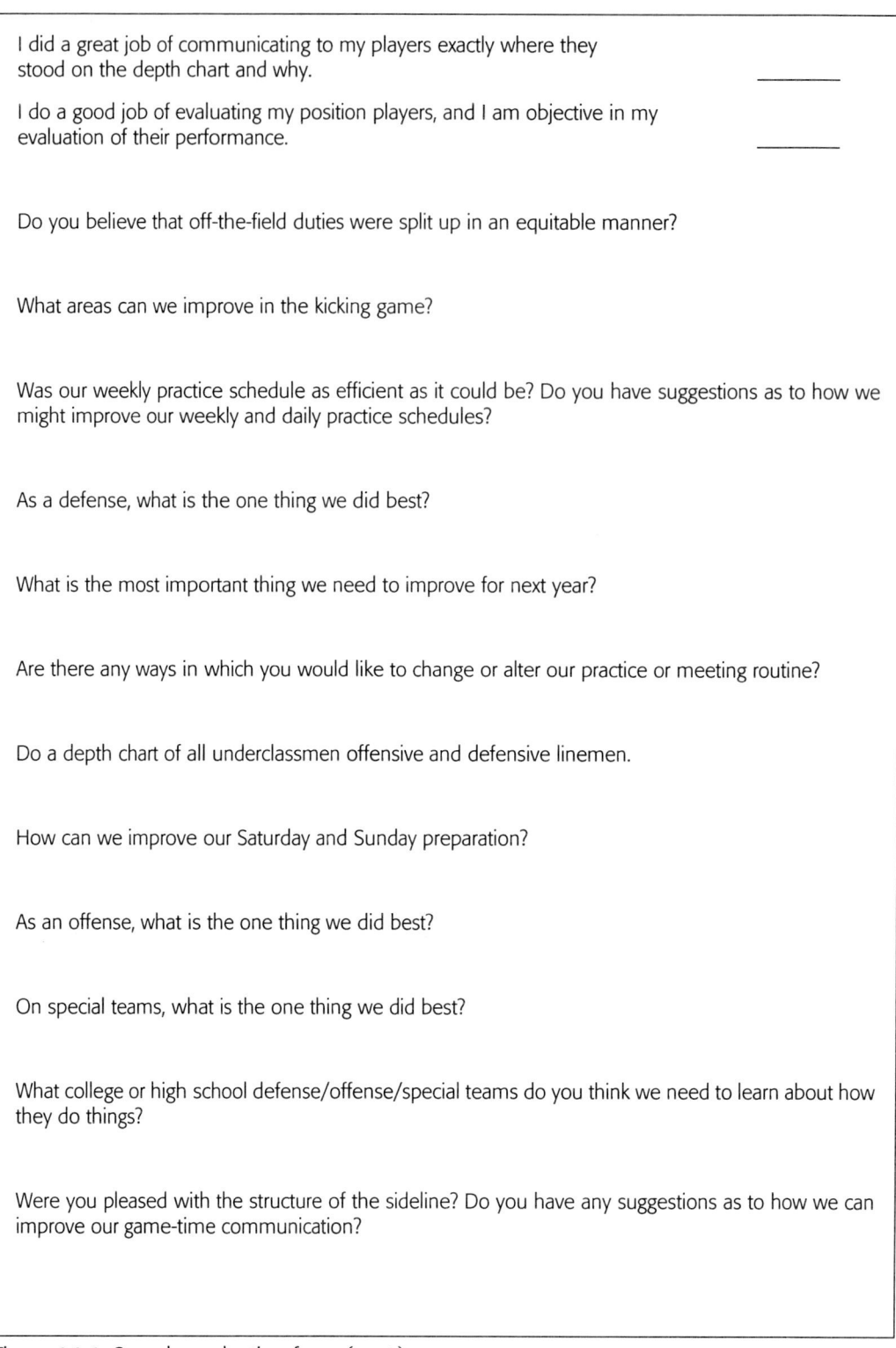

What college or high school defense/offense/special teams do you think we need to learn about how they do things?

Were you pleased with the structure of the sideline? Do you have any suggestions as to how we can improve our game-time communication?

Figure 14-1. Sample evaluation form (cont.)

SECTION 4

THE OFF-SEASON: GET IT GOING AGAIN

The off-season is a time for rest and relaxation—yeah, right! The off-season is the start of the next season. Many coaches race to get started on the off-season plan, the weight training, the running, the skill development, the team-building and bonding, and the recruiting. Make sure to take the time needed to be ready to give 100 percent for the next season.

Remember to help the athletes learn how to compete and to have fun. Help them learn how to make decisions and to make a difference. Make your off-season an experience that any young person would want to be a part of.

15

Build Up and Train Your Next Team

Tip #70: Develop a team website.

Having a team website gives your athletic program validity. The website does not have to be done by an outside company. Developing a team website can be delegated to technology savvy assistant coach or a student in a computer class. Calendars, pictures, videos, blogs, camp forms, announcements, and important links can be among the items placed on a website.

It will be important to get approval from your administration to have a website hosted on the school district website. The technology department will have to approve any format used for the website.

The website can be customized in many different ways. School colors, logos, and mascots can be used. It's a good idea to update the website every few days to keep it current, which will help players, parents, and fans be more interested in the content of your website.

The website can also be used for parents and fans to purchase pictures, videos, fundraising items, and even spirit wear. It is also good to have a blog or message board on the website to make available daily or weekly updates.

Tip #71: Take regular team outings to foster positive relationships.

Team outings are opportunities to build team camaraderie. Team outing ideas could include: movies, meals, paintball, amusement parks, bowling, or anything else you can think of that your athletes would be interested in. The outings should generally not be overnight trips and should be in close proximity to the school to save on transportation costs.

It's a good idea to develop the team outing schedule well ahead of time, and administrative approval for the outings is vital. It's a good idea to have the players give input into where to take outings. The person in charge will need to contact any business the team will be visiting to make arrangements to accommodate any large group. Transportation and meals will need to be planned for as well. Recruiting parents and coaches to help with supervision is important.

The outing is a great way to help players connect with each other and develop trusting relationships with one another. Team chemistry is a vital part to the success of a team, and doing positive, fun things in the off-season is a great way to develop team chemistry.

Tip #72: Develop a team video game tournament.

A video game tournament can be an opportunity for the athletes to compete against other athletes and coaches, as well as have a great time together. Set up a tournament for all players and coaches to participate in a specific game, such as a major new football video game that is released near the beginning of football season. Each player and each coach picks a team to "play" with during the tournament. The coaches set up a tournament bracket, and each player tries to win each game against his teammates to win the tournament. The tournament continues until each team has been eliminated. To play the games, players will need to bring in video game players, and the coaches will need to secure TVs and video projectors. It's a good idea to have the tournament in one place, like a gym. Players that are eliminated from the tournament can watch their teammates that are still playing, or they can play exhibition games at the other end of the gym.

Tip #73: Develop games that will help your players improve their football skills while playing a game for fun.

A great way to keep interest in football is to make sure the athletes are having fun. One way to keep the athletes having fun is to have them compete against each other in games that aren't the specific sports, but develop sport-specific skills. An example of this would be to have quarterbacks throw the football at the basketball rim as a contest. Figure 15-1 shows the set-up for the quarterback target practice game.

Quarterback Target Practice Game

Who: Three or four quarterbacks compete at a time

What: Quarterback target practice

Where: Basketball gym

When: Any time of year, in-season or off-season

Why: Improve quarterback accuracy, strengthen quarterback arm, compete

Notes: The quarterback who is throwing will stand on the free-throw line and face the basketball hoop on the opposite end of the floor. The quarterback will attempt to throw the football into the basket. The quarterback's partner will be on the other end of the floor. He will get the rebound, get set with the football on the free-throw line, and throw the football back, aiming at the opposite basketball hoop. The game continues until the first quarterback reaches 15 points. Points are awarded as follows: backboard = 1, square = 2, net = 2, rim = 3, in the basket = 4.

Figure 15-1. Procedure for quarterback target practice game

Tip #74: Take your team to a college or professional practice.

Almost all young athletes dream of some day becoming a college or professional athlete. Taking your team to a college or professional practice helps keep those dreams alive. It's great to see your athletes be kids and become fans of the local college or professional team. It's important for young people to identify with these athletes.

Additionally, if you take your team to a college practice, the athletes can see what the facilities are like and the athletes can find out what it takes academically and athletically to become a student-athlete at the school you visit. This visit is also a good time to see what successful athletes do at practice, how they finish drills, and how they compete. Many times, the high school does the same drills as a college. Your players can see how the drill should be done.

Tip #75: Develop a daily warm-up program.

The off-season is the time to make adjustments to the daily warm-up program. It's important to have a daily warm-up that is an efficient use of time, warms the players up without wearing them out, and builds spirit among the team. After developing a sound, daily warm-up program, put it on paper, and then videotape the athletes performing the warm-up. By videotaping the warm-up, it will help maintain the integrity of the warm-up over time.

It's a good idea to get players input for the warm-up, since the players will feel fresh and sharp or tired and worn out from the warm-up. The warm-up should last no more than 10 to 15 minutes, and could be as short as eight minutes. The main goal of the warm-up is to reduce the chance for injury to muscles and joints, by increasing blood flow to the muscles and joints.

After the exercises are decided on, they need to be put in the correct order and then practiced by the players. It's important that the warm-up flows naturally and the players don't have to think too much to remember what the next exercise is. Writing down the exercises and where the athletes are to be when doing the exercises is important. Videotaping the warm-up will make it easier for new athletes to watch the warm-up on video and be able to fit in more easily. The video will also help new coaches learn the warm-up procedure more quickly.

Tip #76: Develop an off-season weight training and athletic movement plan for your team.

The off-season is when the next team is developed athletically. It is important to evaluate what movements are being done, what movements are needed for play, and what improvements need to be made in the overall athletic ability of the next team. A sample workout plan is shown in Figures 15-2 through 15-6.

Routine 1

- Field/floor
- Bounding on two feet, left, right
- Angle bounding on two feet, left, right
- Single-leg angle bound with pause
- Split stride bounding
- Quick angle, on one and two feet
- Bounding strides
- Single leg lateral bounding
- Bench hops with single-leg landing plus sprint (jump off two feet, land on one, run lateral)
- Tuck jumps
- Boxes or hurdles on overspeed day

Routine 2

- Bleachers
- Quick hops, angle on one foot
- Angle on one foot
- Bounding
- Lateral on one and two feet

Figure 15-2. Sample running workout from a four-day lifting workout

Sample Day One Lifting Sheet

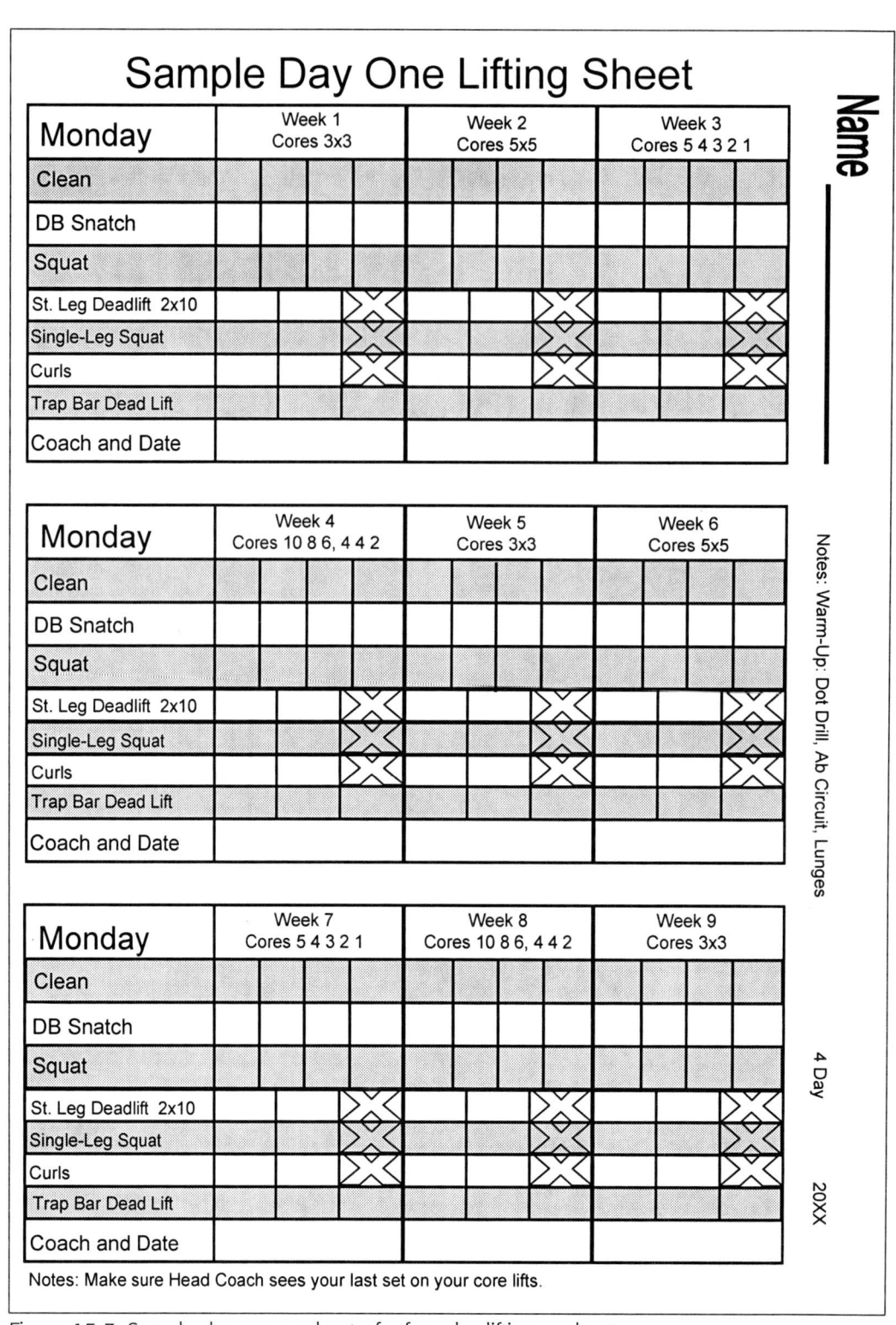

Name

Notes: Warm-Up: Dot Drill, Ab Circuit, Lunges

4 Day 20XX

Monday

	Week 1 Cores 3x3	Week 2 Cores 5x5	Week 3 Cores 5 4 3 2 1
Clean			
DB Snatch			
Squat			
St. Leg Deadlift 2x10			
Single-Leg Squat			
Curls			
Trap Bar Dead Lift			
Coach and Date			

Monday

	Week 4 Cores 10 8 6, 4 4 2	Week 5 Cores 3x3	Week 6 Cores 5x5
Clean			
DB Snatch			
Squat			
St. Leg Deadlift 2x10			
Single-Leg Squat			
Curls			
Trap Bar Dead Lift			
Coach and Date			

Monday

	Week 7 Cores 5 4 3 2 1	Week 8 Cores 10 8 6, 4 4 2	Week 9 Cores 3x3
Clean			
DB Snatch			
Squat			
St. Leg Deadlift 2x10			
Single-Leg Squat			
Curls			
Trap Bar Dead Lift			
Coach and Date			

Notes: Make sure Head Coach sees your last set on your core lifts.

Figure 15-3. Sample day one workout of a four-day lifting workout

Sample Day Two Lifting Sheet

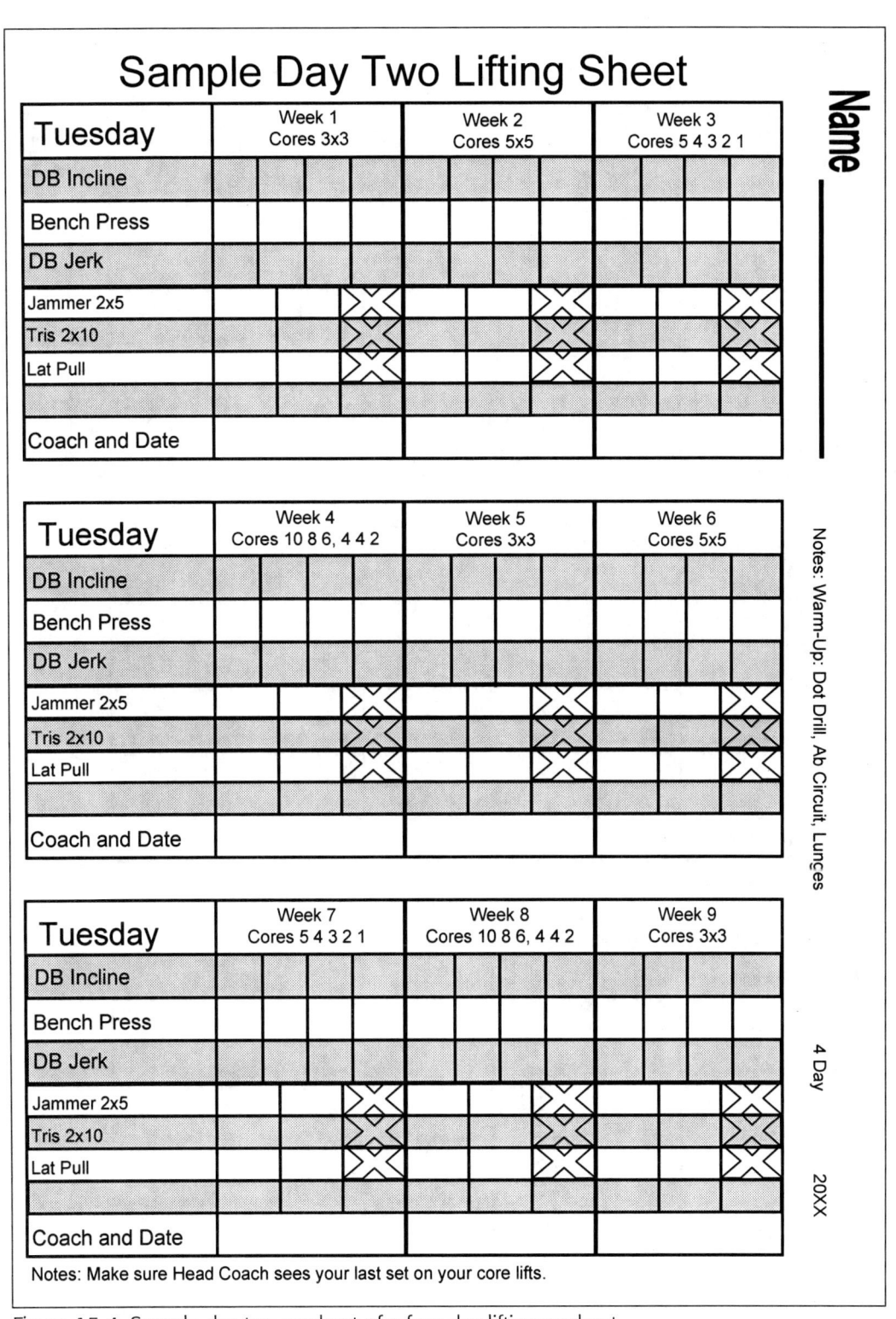

Name

Tuesday	Week 1 Cores 3x3	Week 2 Cores 5x5	Week 3 Cores 5 4 3 2 1
DB Incline			
Bench Press			
DB Jerk			
Jammer 2x5			
Tris 2x10			
Lat Pull			
Coach and Date			

Tuesday	Week 4 Cores 10 8 6, 4 4 2	Week 5 Cores 3x3	Week 6 Cores 5x5
DB Incline			
Bench Press			
DB Jerk			
Jammer 2x5			
Tris 2x10			
Lat Pull			
Coach and Date			

Notes: Warm-Up: Dot Drill, Ab Circuit, Lunges

Tuesday	Week 7 Cores 5 4 3 2 1	Week 8 Cores 10 8 6, 4 4 2	Week 9 Cores 3x3
DB Incline			
Bench Press			
DB Jerk			
Jammer 2x5			
Tris 2x10			
Lat Pull			
Coach and Date			

4 Day 20XX

Notes: Make sure Head Coach sees your last set on your core lifts.

Figure 15-4. Sample day two workout of a four-day lifting workout

Sample Day Three Lifting Sheet

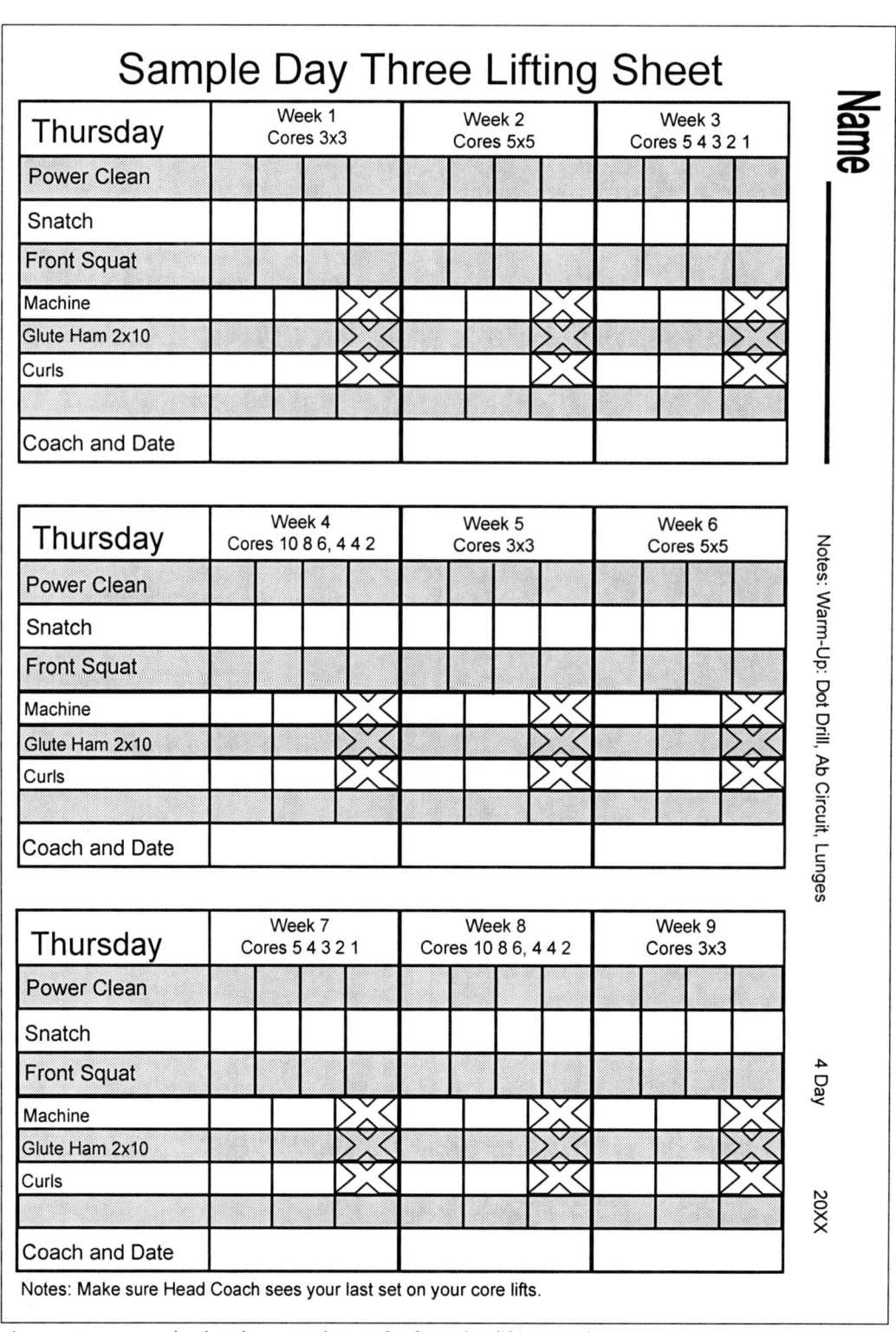

Name

Notes: Warm-Up: Dot Drill, Ab Circuit, Lunges

4 Day — 20XX

Thursday	Week 1 Cores 3x3	Week 2 Cores 5x5	Week 3 Cores 5 4 3 2 1
Power Clean			
Snatch			
Front Squat			
Machine			
Glute Ham 2x10			
Curls			
Coach and Date			

Thursday	Week 4 Cores 10 8 6, 4 4 2	Week 5 Cores 3x3	Week 6 Cores 5x5
Power Clean			
Snatch			
Front Squat			
Machine			
Glute Ham 2x10			
Curls			
Coach and Date			

Thursday	Week 7 Cores 5 4 3 2 1	Week 8 Cores 10 8 6, 4 4 2	Week 9 Cores 3x3
Power Clean			
Snatch			
Front Squat			
Machine			
Glute Ham 2x10			
Curls			
Coach and Date			

Notes: Make sure Head Coach sees your last set on your core lifts.

Figure 15-5. Sample day three workout of a four-day lifting workout

Sample Day Four Lifting Sheet

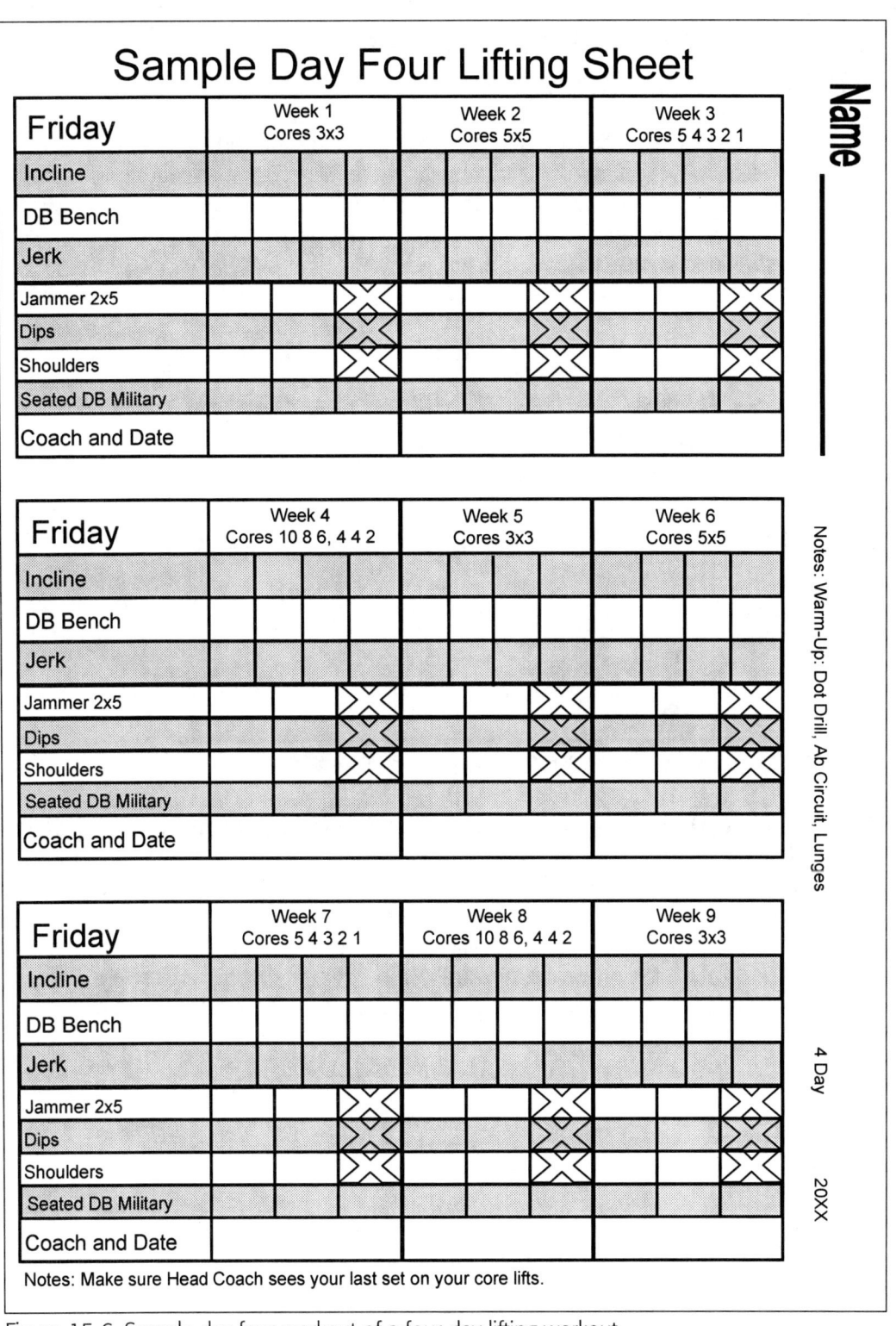

Name

Friday	Week 1 Cores 3x3			Week 2 Cores 5x5			Week 3 Cores 5 4 3 2 1		
Incline									
DB Bench									
Jerk									
Jammer 2x5			✕			✕			✕
Dips			✕			✕			✕
Shoulders			✕			✕			✕
Seated DB Military									
Coach and Date									

Friday	Week 4 Cores 10 8 6, 4 4 2			Week 5 Cores 3x3			Week 6 Cores 5x5		
Incline									
DB Bench									
Jerk									
Jammer 2x5			✕			✕			✕
Dips			✕			✕			✕
Shoulders			✕			✕			✕
Seated DB Military									
Coach and Date									

Notes: Warm-Up: Dot Drill, Ab Circuit, Lunges

Friday	Week 7 Cores 5 4 3 2 1			Week 8 Cores 10 8 6, 4 4 2			Week 9 Cores 3x3		
Incline									
DB Bench									
Jerk									
Jammer 2x5			✕			✕			✕
Dips			✕			✕			✕
Shoulders			✕			✕			✕
Seated DB Military									
Coach and Date									

Notes: Make sure Head Coach sees your last set on your core lifts.

4 Day 20XX

Figure 15-6. Sample day four workout of a four-day lifting workout

Tip #77: Develop an off-season sport-specific improvement plan for each position.

The off-season sport-specific improvement plan for each position goes hand in hand with the off-season weight training and athletic movement plan. Evaluations will need to be done for each returning player and compared athletically to what a successful athlete will be able to do movement-wise by position. A sample list of expected movements and lifts is shown in Figure 15-7.

	Skilled	**Lineman**
Squat	365-405	405-500
Clean	245-305	275-345
Bench	225-275	265-325
Snatch	175-215	195-235
40	4.5-4.9	4.9-5.4
Pro	4.1-4.3	4.2-4.5
Vertical	27-35+	24-29+

Figure 15-7. Sample list of expected movements and lifts

Tip #78: Take attendance at all off-season activities.

Attendance is not mandatory for off-season activities. Many state activities associations do not allow off-season workouts or meetings to be mandatory. It's still a good reference to take attendance for all off-season activities. Using attendance is a good way to reward athletes. Taking attendance communicates to the athletes that what they are showing up for is important. Microsoft Excel is a good program to use for attendance.

Tip #79: Develop a player handbook.

The off-season is the time to develop a player handbook. Make sure to use input from player and post-season coach evaluations. The player handbook needs to list all expectations and responsibilities of players.

The player handbook should be a professional looking document, and it should include team rules as well as consequences. The handbook can also include player-lettering policy, evaluation procedures, and anything else that pertains to the responsibilities of a player in the program. The handbook should be typed in a word processor so that it can be edited and amended easily. The coach should remember that any changes made to player expectations or team rules will need to be emphasized the next season for players to remember. Also, anything regarding consequences should be approved by administration.

Tip #80: Develop a leadership council and training.

One of our most important jobs as coaches is to develop leaders, not only for our own team, but also for the society of tomorrow. It is a good idea to either select a group of players or have the team vote for leaders to serve on a leadership council. Once selected, begin to train the leaders in leadership skills. In addition to training the leaders, give them responsibilities as well as input. Leaders can be trained in meetings before school, after school, or on the weekends. They can also be trained during lunch or a study hall.

The head coach needs to do research on leadership and the best way to teach leadership to team leaders. It's a good idea to choose about 10 percent of the team be on the leadership council. Again, the head coach needs to decide what is important to the team by developing and sharing the philosophy of the team with the leadership council and to the team. The training of leaders should be no more than 30 minutes at a time, and should not last more than two months. It's a good rule of thumb to develop a lesson each week.

The leadership council will be leaders by example; they will also serve as extra eyes and ears for the coaches. The leadership council can help make decisions, like what color socks the team will wear for a game, or what they would like to eat for the next pre-game meal. The members of the council must remember that they are representatives of the team.

16

Educate and Encourage Parents

Tip #81: Develop a moms squad for program support.

The mothers of your players can make great allies. The mothers are good at fundraising and organizing. By developing a moms squad in the off-season, you as the head coach can delegate more tasks to save you time during the season.

Many moms squads run just like booster clubs, with officers and committees. To develop a successful moms squad, it would be good to set up the structure of the group ahead of time and set the priorities for the group up front. The moms will need to know what their roles and responsibilities are. The mothers of players are sometimes the best recruiters of help within the community. The moms squad can take care of pre-game meals, the concession stand, and anything else that the coach needs help with.

To start the moms squad, the coach should have an invitation to meet with the moms to help the football program. The coach can explain, during the meeting, how he would like the organization to be set up, and what needs to be done. Keep in mind that, to many workers, the burden is light. The coach can provide goals or just general guidance to get the group started. After the initial meeting, the coach will want to set up a schedule for regular meetings for the moms squad. It's important to publicize the work of the women and the appreciation for their dedication and help.

The moms squad will need to have a financial plan and will need to be legal. All money must be official and accounted for by more than one person. Financial statements must be available to the public.

Tip #82: Develop a parent handbook to be shared in the pre-season.

The parent handbook is a good way to sell the priorities of your program. The parent handbook will help parents get an idea of what is important to you and what they can expect from you and your coaching staff.

The parent handbook also helps educate the parents on what their responsibilities are. In addition, the parent handbook will help the parents understand the best way to support their child and the program. Topics for a parent handbook include the following:

- Participation criteria
- Academics
- Relationships
- Team concept and philosophy
- Leadership
- Program priorities
- Communication
- Diet
- Criticism
- Donations
- Other areas of help
- Rules
- Signature

Tip #83: Hold a parent meeting on high school eligibility and college recruitment.

The parent meeting is important to help parents understand two main points. The first point to cover is how the parents can help their child attain and maintain their high school eligibility. The second point to educate parents on is how their child can be recruited to become a college student athlete. A sample agenda from a parent eligibility and college recruiting meeting is as follows:

- High school eligibility academic and citizenship
- Types of colleges and affiliations: NCAA (all divisions), NAIA, junior colleges
    - ✓ Academic requirements of each
    - ✓ Scholarship opportunities of each (how many, full or partial)
    - ✓ Athletic requirements of each
- NCAA Clearinghouse: Registration and requirements
- High school academic timeline
    - ✓ When to take the ACT/SAT
    - ✓ What is the ACT/SAT
    - ✓ Registration
    - ✓ Cost
    - ✓ Preparation aids
    - ✓ Questions
- Developing a marketing plan for your child
    - ✓ Services
    - ✓ Recruiting questions
    - ✓ Signing dates and questions

Tip #84: Create a quarterly newsletter to keep parents informed.

A quarterly newsletter is an excellent way to communicate with parents. Copies of the newsletter can also be sent to administrators, board members, booster club members, and anyone else you can think of. The newsletter can list upcoming events, calendar, new top lifting marks, updated top academic performances, as well as anything else that needs to be communicated. The newsletter is a great way to brag on your kids and your program. A sample of a newsletter is shown in Figure 16-3.

Tip #85: Send appreciation notes home to parents, bragging on their kids.

The appreciation notes are a great way to create a positive relationship between the coaches of the school and the parents. Parents are always happy to hear when their child is doing a good job. The more you can brag on the work their child is doing, the better you, as the coach, will look.

The appreciation notes can be on school or official team postcards, or they can be purchased blank in bulk. It's a good idea to send out 5 to 10 notes a week so there aren't too many to write at a time. This approach will help the coach do a better job with each note written. The notes need to be personal; sometimes, a coach could list the amount of weight the athlete lifted last week or an improvement on a skill. It's important to write the notes very regularly, especially in the off-season, as the in-season time is not very easily accessible when the coach is busy doing game plans and watching film.

UNION FOOTBALL
Union High School Football Spring Newsletter

Dates to Remember:
- ACT
  - Next Test Date: April 12
  - Registration Deadline: March 8–21 (late fee may apply)
- Team Trip to Indoor Football Game April 12, 7:00 PM Cost will be $10.00 plus food money
- Parent Meeting On Recruitment April 15, 6:00 PM in the Fine Arts Center

20XX Schedule

Jamboree @ Farmington	8-22
@Rckwd Summit	8-29
Poplar Bluff	9-5
St James	9-12
@Herman	9-19
@Jeff City Helias	9-26
Sullivan	10-3
Owensville	10-10
@Hillsboro	10-17
@Pacific	10-24
St. Clair	10-30

Union School District
123 Street
Union, MO 63084

Calling All Parents

We invite all Wildcat parents to take a close look at the Union Wildcat Football Calendar for 20XX. We have numerous opportunities for you to participate in future Wildcat success.

The Union coaches appreciate all the hard work and involvement parents put into this program and would like to extend an invitation to join us for some new and unique activities.

Included this year will be a meeting to help parents understand college recruiting. The Mom's Football Clinic will be designed to help answer questions they may have about how we play the game, what your sons' responsibilities are, and the ins and outs of officiating by an actual official. Also, watch for details about the upcoming Wildcat Parent Player Float Trip in June.

Union Football Continues Winning Ways in the Weight Room

Weight Sessions
Monday-Friday
6:40-7:50am
or
Mon, Wed, Fri
3:00-4:20pm

Over 60 young men continue to pay the price for success through weight and grades. Despite the temptation of spring distractions, the Wildcats remain focused on repeating a District 10 Championship and beyond.

Football championships are won in the weight room as much as on the field. It is important for players <u>and parents</u> to understand the importance of the weight and running sessions. These sessions prepare an athlete's body to compete and also prevent injury. The Union football weight training program is specifically designed by the coaches for the team to develop lasting relationships and meet the specific needs of the student athletes.

Listed below are the top five lifters for each category and the top 5 GPAs of students currently participating in Wildcat Football.

Top 5 Squat		Top 5 Bench		Top 5 Power Clean		Top 5 Lifters		Top 5 GPAs	
James B.	461	Adam A.	312	Jarred C.	353	Adam A.	1032	Michael Y.	
Adam A.	439	Jordan W.	307	Jordan W.	327	James B.	1029	Steven P.	
Josh P.	421	Patrick G.	278	Jon M.	326	Jordan W.	1016	Dylan M.	
Steve S.	418	Tommy K.	277	James B.	301	Steve S.	984	Lucas P.	
Nathan H.	407	Malcolm S.	275	Colter J.	301	Jon M.	961	Colter J.	

ADRESS
HERE

Figure 16-3. Sample newsletter

UNION WILDCAT FOOTBALL CALENDAR 20XX
2/11/XX Tentative

Union High School
123 Street
Union, MO 63084
123-456-7890

Or Call Head Football
Coach Brent Eckley
Cell (555) 111-2222

20XX Schedule

Jambree @ Farmington	8-22
@Rockwood Summit	8-29
Poplar Bluff	9-5
St James	9-12
@Herman	9-19
@Jeff City Helias	9-26
Sullivan	10-3
Owensville	10-10
@Hillsboro	10-17
@Pacific	10-24
St Clair	10-30

For comments or recommendations about this newsletter contact Coach Jones.
jones@school.email

December	Off-Season Phase I
January 3-March 21	Off-Season Phase II
March 24-May 16	Off-Season Phase III
March 25-May 15	Open Gym Tues/Thurs Mornings 6:30-7:00 AM
April 12	Team Trip to Indoor Football Game 7:00 PM
April 15	Parent Meeting on College Recruitment 6:00 PM
April 2-May 14	Open Field Wednesdays 5:30-7:00 PM
May 28-July 23	Summer School Weight Training (See calendar for times)
May 28	7 on 7 With Webster Groves
May 28-July 23	Open Field 10:00-11:30 AM WEDNESDAYS ONLY
June 8-12	Union High School Team Camp 4:00-8:30 PM
June 13-14	Washington Team Camp 12:00-8:00 PM
June 5	7 on 7 Passing League 6:00 PM @ TBD
June 19	7 on 7 Passing League 6:00 PM @ TBD
June 26	7 on 7 Passing League 6:00 PM @ TBD
June 27-28	Parent Player Float Trip
July 10	7 on 7 Passing League 6:00 PM @ TBD
July 11	Mom's Football Clinic 6:00 PM
July 13-17	Union High School Team Camp 4:00-8:30 PM
July 23	Last Day of Summer School Weight Training
July 24- August 10	Vacation
August 7-8	Coaches' Meetings Time TBD
August 11	1ST Official Practice 3:00-8:30 PM
August 14	1ST Day in Full Pads 3:00-8:30 PM
August 15	Media Day: HS: 3:00 PM
	Practice 4:30-7:00 PM
	Lock-In 9:00 PM – 8:00 AM
August 16	Scrimmage 8:30-11:30 AM
	Parent Meeting/Family Meal 12:00-1:30 PM
	Booster Club Meeting/Meal 6:00 PM
August 22	Jamboree @ Farmington 6:00 PM
August 29	1ST Game @ Rockwood Summit
September 1	Labor Day: Practice 3:00-6:30 PM
October 30	Game 10 vs St. Clair on Thursday
	(we will practice each day after this date, generally in the PM)
November 5	1ST Round Play-off Game
November 10	2ND Round Play-off Game
November 15	3RD Round Play-off Game
November 22	4TH Round Play-off Game

Two Union Seniors Continue Careers in College

Two Union senior football players accepted scholarships to continue playing football next year at the collegiate level.

After outstanding performances by senior wide receiver/defensive back Chris S. and senior wide receiver/linebacker Jed N., the Lindenwood Lions have invited these players to join their squad next year.

N. contributed to Union's high-flying aerial show with 84 receptions for 1500+ yards. On defense he added 95 tackles, 15 tackles for loss, 6 sacks, and 4 interceptions to his career totals.

S. provided equally impressive numbers on offense, adding 98 receptions for 1200+ yards. He was also pressed into service to shore up the Wildcat secondary throughout the year.

Both of these young men will prove difficult to replace, having left their mark on this program. As part of the 20XX offense, they will share in the following state team records:

1st All-Time YPG

1st Pass Yards Per Game

Figure 16-3. Sample newsletter (cont.)

17

Continue to Connect With and Recruit the Community

Tip #86: Run a youth league.

Your off-season provides the most time to run a league for your youth. A youth league is another excellent way to connect with your future players. Additionally, running a youth league provides opportunities for your high school athletes to work with younger athletes. Running a flag football league during the off-season is a great way to develop interest in the sport. All kids get the opportunity to pass, catch, and run. Figure 17-1 shows a sample informational letter for flag football.

Tip #87: Provide clinics for your youth team coaches.

Youth coaches, in general, are not educators, and they're not coaches by trade. Youth coaches either coach because they have a son on the team, they love the sport and this is as close as they can get to playing again, or they are truly interested in helping young people have a great experience with sports.

Having clinics for youth coaches gives the head coach more control and input for the program. The off-season provides more time to develop a clinic schedule. Make sure to keep clinics short, as most youth coaches attending the clinic will have already worked a full day. Have an agenda, and stay on schedule.

Again, the clinic allows the coach to present schemes that the high school uses. It also allows the head coach to teach a beginning drill progression for each position and specific necessary skills.

[Name] High School 20XX Spring Flag Football Season
For boys and girls in grades K-8. Sign up as a team or as individuals

[Name] High School Football will offer Spring Flag Football, March 21 through April 25. One game will be played each Saturday with games starting at 10 a.m., 11 a.m., and 12 p.m. If we have too many teams, we will also play games on Sunday afternoons with games beginning at 1 p.m. The league will consist of six games. Games will be played at [Name] High School. Practices are scheduled by coaches. Players can be from any school district. Divisions are by grades: K-1, 2-3, 4-5, and 6-8. Teams can have both boys and girls. The fee is $50 and will include an NFL flag football jersey to keep. Each additional child is half price ($25.00).

All registration forms must be postmarked by February 27, 20XX. No forms will be accepted after that. *No exceptions!* Coach your child's team, and that child plays for free. Send in your check, and it will be returned at the end of the season. Let coach John Coach know if you want to coach.

Team Registration: Designate a coach, and form a team with a limit of 10 players. Give your registration form and check to your coach. The coach will mail or deliver the forms and checks to the high school to John Coach. Teams will choose their NFL team, first come preferences.

Individual Registration: Fill out the registration form and mail the form with your check to the address provided. You will be placed on a team according to your grade. Please make sure that you write your email address clearly and legibly. Please send your flag registration form and check to:

    [Name] High School
    1 High School Drive
    Anywhere, USA 12345

*Please make check payable to "[Name] High School Football."
*Questions: jcoach@highschool.k12.mo.us
Registration Deadline: Must be postmarked by February 27, 20XX

Student's Name _____

School _____ Grade _____

Mother's Name _____ Father's Name _____

Mailing Address _____

City _____ Zip _____ Phone number _____

Parent's email (neatly please) _____

Cell/Alternate Number _____

Student's date of birth _____ Size: YM YL AS AM AL AXL A2XL

Coaches need to pay registration fee, but it will be reimbursed when equipment is returned. If coaching:

Cell phone_____ Work Phone_____

    I give permission for my child to participate in the NFL Flag Football program. I will not hold the league, coaches, or school district liable for possible injuries that may occur during the program.

Parent's Printed Name _____

Parent's Signature _____

Team Registration Only: Coach _____

NFL Team Preference:

First Choice _____ Second Choice _____

Figure 17-1. Sample flag football informational letter

Tip #88: Develop a service-learning project for your team to take part in.

Participation in a service-learning project is an important way to help young people learn how to give back. A service-learning project will need to be well-organized and publicized. The project could be working on a house-building project, adopting a road or street, helping with a landscape project for the city or school district, or helping at the local animal shelter of the community. Identify a need, and then work to fulfill it. Most service-learning projects will be more beneficial if the students actually do something physical and the students can see the job they have completed. In addition to helping your team learn how to do for others, the service-learning project helps the community see that the coach and program aren't just out for themselves, but are willing to help others and give back.

To get started, the coach can contact the school district, city, or even the state to research possible service-learning projects. The coach must get administrative approval, and then he can get input from the leadership council on which project would be best for the team. The project could be done during the school year on weekends or in the evening, or it could be done during the summer months. Supervision must be handled by having assistant coaches and parents help. Parents might also have to help provide transportation, if needed. For most service-learning projects, parents must also sign a waiver for their child to participate. The coach must make sure to publicize the work done and have a celebration time for the team and any volunteers at the conclusion of the project.

18

Organize and Train Your Staff

Tip #89: Create and develop a playbook.

The off-season is the time to work on the playbook. Remember to include your assistant coaches when developing the playbook. The off-season provides the much-needed time to develop schemes to implement the following season. The off-season is also the time to do research on possible changes in the schemes you already use.

Playbooks can be developed in sport-specific playbook development software or in a program like Microsoft Word or PowerPoint. A sample page of a playbook is shown in Figure 18-1.

Tip #90: Develop a staff handbook.

Following the postseason staff evaluation, you should have ample feedback to develop a staff handbook. In addition to developing policies and procedures, as well as staff responsibilities, a staff handbook is a great way to maintain leverage on your staff. By having a staff handbook with a signature page, all staff members are committing to do what is listed in the staff handbook.

Points to include in the staff handbook could include: coach demeanor, off-field behavior, dealing with parents, the administration, the community, and the players, how to interact with other coaches, time schedules, and what events require attendance, as well as many others.

Option

Philosophy: This is our option play. We will use this play to attack blitzing defenses. The option is a good play to get us to the perimeter quickly.

WRs	Playside: stalk, backside: cutoff.
F	Drop step, run the bubble, and look for the ball quickly. Get width to isolate the defensive end.
PST	Even front: double with the PSG. Odd front: climb to playside LB. Just like shovel.
PSG	Even front: double with the PST. Odd front: double with the center to the playside LB. Just like shovel.
CENTER	Zone block to the playside versus all fronts. Just like shovel. Train, bus, zebra.
BSG	Zone block to the playside versus all fronts. Just like shovel. Train, bus zebra.
BST	Zone block to the playside versus all fronts. Just like shovel. Train, bus, zebra.
QB	After catching the snap, directly attack the inside of the defensive end. If he commits to you, pitch. If not, keep the ball and turn it up.

Option versus 3-3

We will change the scheme vs. 3-3. We will block the end & pitch off of the pslb.

Option versus 3-2

Option versus 4-1

Option versus 4-2

Option versus Bear

Figure 18-1. Playbook sample page

Tip #91: Research and purchase video-editing, statistic, and tendency programs.

The purchase of these software programs is not cheap, but it's an important investment in your program. Purchasing the right software program will help your staff work more efficiently. The right software program will also allow your staff to be more involved in video, statistics, and tendencies. Research is available to help make a decision. The need for this software is one reason that fundraising is so important, no matter what size school you coach at.

Video-editing programs can cost hundreds of dollars to hundreds of thousands of dollars. The program could be software only, or it could also include hardware, like computers and cameras. Staff input will be important. The program you purchase will need to be used by more than one person, in most cases. Make sure to receive administrative approval ahead of time to spend money on this product. Additionally, practice on the software is best done well ahead of the season, so coaches aren't still trying to figure out the program during the season, which will hurt coach efficiency. Some other factors to consider include how much storage the converted video will take up, what customer support is provided, how long free updates are provided, whether the video can be used on the Internet, and what types of computers are required to use the product.

Tip #92: Go to clinics, and take your staff.

Clinics serve two main purposes. The first purpose is to gather information. When at a clinic, a typical coach will spend the majority of his time sitting in clinic sessions, learning more about a scheme or technique the program already employs, or a scheme that the program is considering adopting.

The second purpose of going to clinics is to network with other coaches. When at a clinic, it's a good idea to talk to other non-presenting coaches who are sitting in the same clinic sessions. Many times, the coaches who are not presenting will know as much about the topic being discussed as the presenter. Sometimes, the information from the non-presenting coach can be a better fit for your program. Always consider speaking with a new coach in each clinic session to enlarge the circle of influence you are working in.

Tip #93: Join local and state coaching associations.

Joining local and state associations is a responsibility of the head coach. This point is important in making sure your staff is connected with other coaches from the area and the state. The associations are only as good as the commitment of the membership. Be involved, and help to make your football program better. Attend meetings, and volunteer your staff to help.

The best way to get involved is to contact the association in the off-season. Make sure you are a member, and then find out if the association has any committee openings. Many state associations also have regional or local associations that serve as committees to the state association. Make sure your school is aware of any responsibilities required by your local and state associations. Most associations have three to five meetings for professional development, all-state selection, or recruiting. The more involved you are, the better prepared you are to help yourself and the students you coach.

Tip #94: Train your staff on how to teach sport skills, how to recruit, and the specifics of the schemes your program uses.

It's a good idea to use the off-season to train your own staff on the cornerstone beliefs of your program. The off-season is the time to sell your staff on your system. It is the time to teach your staff how to watch film, what the read progression is for your quarterback on a specific route, or what the drill progression should be for open field tackling.

The off-season can also be a great opportunity to help staff members gain valuable knowledge to expand their role on your staff. As the head coach, you could use the off-season to help a staff member become a valuable asset on game nights from the press box, by watching film together and developing a set script of things to look for and things to communicate from the press box.

Tip #95: Invest in professional development by paying to have a coach come in to talk to your staff.

In addition to taking your staff to clinics, sometimes it's in the best interest of your staff to pay a coach to come in for a clinic with you and your staff. This arrangement allows the head coach the opportunity to schedule around the staff schedules. This approach also allows for a greater level of teaching and learning. Many coaches are interested in helping other coaches in the off-season.

The best way to arrange this clinic is to call on coaches you are interested in having come to share with you. Work out a schedule, based on the coach's availability and your staff's availability. Set up the time, find out what the coach needs to present, have it prepared, and make sure you identify what you want to learn. Make sure to decide on the amount to be paid to the coach, and find a way to fundraise for the money or have it donated. Make sure to get this type of professional development approved by administration.

Tip #96: Purchase position-oriented T-shirts for coaches and players.

Purchasing T-shirts is a fairly routine job, but when staff members take pride in the position they coach, it's a good idea to help the coach and position group develop a positive identity. Allow the position coach to work with his players to develop the artwork for the shirt.

Athletes generally wear their team shirts with pride; the same can be said for position-specific shirts. This use of shirts is also another great way to bring your team closer together and to help individual players develop pride in the specific unit of the team in which they contribute. This shirt is different than the game-day shirt or the seasonal theme shirt; it's only for the linebackers, or only the quarterbacks. This approach helps kids feel included regardless of their age or grade.

SECTION 5

THINGS TO DO ALL YEAR LONG

Coaching used to be from the first day a team could practice until the last scheduled game. Those were the days that the team had "a" coach, and the coach would generally coach three sports.

Today, it's different. So many of our young people are specializing in one sport, the coach must supervise off-season activities, oversee strength and conditioning, take the team to pre-season camps, and manage recruitment.

Today's coach must continue to connect with each of his athletes and help fill the gap created by the lack of parental involvement or help give direction to the athlete that suffers from too much parental involvement.

It's not easy to coach today. It's a yearlong job, but if you're a "coach," it's not really a job; it's what you are.

19

Keys to Maintaining Your Success—It Never Ends

Tip #97: Delegate to your staff.

One of the most important keys to any successful head coach is his ability to delegate. Allow assistant coaches the freedom to take on new tasks that improve your program. Give assistant coaches responsibility and authority. Responsibilities that can be delegated include the following:
- Position and level
- Equipment room
- Locker room supervision and clean-up
- Field equipment
- Film
- Eligibility
- Player equipment and uniforms
- Bulletin boards
- Post practice make-ups/conditioning
- Roster
- Headsets
- Pre-game warm-up duties
- Game responsibilities
- Halftime responsibilities
- Post-game responsibilities
- Kicking game responsibilities
- Weight room
- Film exchange
- Scout team responsibilities
- Scouting report and game plan responsibilities

Tip #98: Send birthday cards to your players.

Sending birthday cards is a cheap and easy way to show care and compassion for your players. It is easy to get a list of all player birthdays from the attendance office at your school. Blank cards can be purchased or school letterhead postcards can be used. Sending a birthday card to a player might be the only way his birthday is recognized by anyone.

Once you have the list of birthdays, make sure to check the list at least once per week. From the list, prepare the birthday cards one time each week, and have them mailed out to the student's home, addressed to the student. Make sure to put something personal on the birthday card.

Tip #99: Order T-shirts, shorts, or sweatshirts every six to eight weeks for players to buy.

Ordering apparel every six to eight weeks keeps the players interested in your program. All players want to wear nice, up-to-date things. Athletes generally feel better about their program when they are wearing nice apparel, and then they have more program pride. Additionally, ordering apparel every six to eight weeks keeps new stuff for assistant coaches, and it is a good way to express thanks for off-season work. Some programs use these apparel orders as program fundraisers, by charging the athletes 20 to 25 percent over the cost of the apparel.

It's a good idea to order shorts at one point and then offer sweatshirts and then T-shirts, rather than ordering the same type of clothing each time or rather than ordering the same color each time. This variety will help players wear their school colors with pride and always feel like they look like the college or pro players. Player input can be a part of what to order and what designs to use. These orders can also help with leadership positions in your program by purchasing the apparel for the top three to five lifters, or leaders or athletes with the highest grade-point average.

Tip #100: Create a bulletin board, and keep it up-to-date to advertise your program.

A bulletin board is a cheap and easy way to advertise your program. The coach can continue to add up-to-date material during the off-season, like college signings, updated top lifter lists, and upcoming camp dates. The coach needs to find a bulletin board in the school that is a high traffic area to use or find a high traffic area to put a bulletin board up. The bulletin board is useless if it is not kept up-to-date.

Tip #101: Recognize your top lifters, runners, good grades, and anything else that can be tracked and rewarded.

Many young people participate in athletics for recognition. Any time the coach can recognize the accomplishments of the athletes, it will help the athletes work harder. It's important to maintain balance when recognizing academics and all types of athletic performance.

In recognizing performance, it's good to publicize the accomplishment as much as possible. Award boards in the weight room, bulletin boards around the school, a newsletter, a website, and the local newspaper can all be used to recognize athletic accomplishments

Bonus Tip: Call players by their first name.

Calling players by their first name is just an everyday thing that shows respect for your players. When communicating with young people, it's important to be sincere. Using an athlete's first name is more personal.

Bonus Tip: Obtain the class schedule of each of your players to track the academic progress of each athlete in your program.

At all times, it's important for the coach to know where each of his athletes are supposed to be throughout the school day. It's also important for the coach to track the academic progress of each athlete. The academic schedule can be obtained from the guidance office, or printed out if the school has an online grading and attendance system.

Bonus Tip: Adopt an elementary classroom to mentor.

Adopting an elementary classroom is a good example of a service-learning project for a high school team. This project also serves as a great connection with the young people of the community as well as a great way to help elementary teachers. Athletes can help with any class subject as well as play with the students during physical education class or recess. The time spent is an excellent investment of time. All young people can use another positive role model. High school students need to be educated on how to behave and why they are adopting the classroom. Inviting the classroom to a home game, and then being able to talk with the athlete either before or after the game can extend the connection.

Any coach wanting to pursue this endeavor should contact the administration from each school to see if schedules can be matched up and if high school students can be out of school for the number of hours required. Transportation will need to be addressed as well. This project can be used as a service-learning project, but it can also be a great stand-alone project for the kids, both young and old, just to offer mentorship.

Bonus Tip: Engage in fundraising for your program all year long.

Fundraising is a responsibility that many coaches have to undertake. If you are in charge of fundraising for your program, try to find ways that give value to the customer for product you are selling. Think of services to provide or creative ways to give community members the opportunity to invest in the program. If you are in charge of fundraising, remember the other coaches from your district are also in charge of their fundraising; don't do the same fundraiser or undercut their fundraiser. Possible fundraising activities include the following:

- Car washes
- Discount card sales
- Magazine sales
- Candy and food sales
- Request for donation letter
- Lift-a-thon
- Rent-a-player
- Youth league
- Youth camp
- Alumni game
- Flag football tournament for youth age to adult age
- Picture sales
- Highlight and game video sales
- T-shirt sales
- Other clothing sales (sweatshirts, jackets etc.)
- Seat license sales
- Golf tournament
- Poker tournament
- Dinner/silent auction 50/50 drawing at games
- Auction game balls
- Auction sideline passes

Bonus Tip: Train leaders, and educate your players on character.

Your main goal as a coach cannot be to win. Your main goal has to mean more than that. Every coach should strive to help the athletes under his direction to learn to make better decisions, to do what's right when no one is watching, to handle adversity and overcome challenges and setbacks, to help other people, to learn to work with and for other people, and to learn how to encourage and care for other people. Additionally, it would be good to teach athletes how to go after what they really want, work extremely hard for a far-off goal, to get athletes to do more than they thought they could, and to be inspired to help other people achieve the same success.

These traits are the things that make athletics valuable. Athletes are different because of the coaches that inspire, teach, and challenge them to be different. Character education should not be foreign to any coach. Athletes don't learn character by being at practice. Coaches have to use those precious few teachable moments to help teach the character traits that will help young people mature into outstanding adults. Following is a list of possible character traits to research and try to develop for high school athletes:

- Attitude
- Goal-setting
- Effort
- Humility
- Honesty
- Vision
- Spirit
- Leadership
- Perseverance
- Habits
- Fairness
- Respect
- Responsibility
- Compassion
- Trust
- Influence
- Integrity
- Communication
- Courage
- Sacrifice
- Servanthood

About the Author

Brent Eckley is the head football coach at Union High School in Union, Missouri, a position he has held since 2005. In that period the Wildcats have won four district championships and three conference championships, and have qualified for the state playoffs five years in a row.

Previous to the 2005 season, Eckley was the head football coach at Montgomery County High School in Montgomery City, Missouri, for five seasons, and finished with the highest winning percentage in the school's history. During his tenure, the Wildcats won three conference and three district championships, winning 28 of their last 33 games under Eckley. Prior to coaching at Montgomery County, Eckley was an assistant coach and the offensive coordinator at Warrensburg High School in Warrensburg, Missouri, from 1997 to 1999. Before coaching in Warrensburg, Eckley's first coaching assignment was as an assistant coach at Hickman Mills High School in Kansas City, Missouri, in 1995 and 1996. Eckley's overall record as a head coach is 90-31.

Eckley played college football in his home state of Iowa at William Penn University in Oskaloosa, Iowa, where he received his bachelor's degree in elementary education. He was a three-year letterman for the Statesmen football team, and was a two-year starter as a defensive lineman.

Known for his explosive offenses, Eckley has coached five different quarterbacks to throw for more than 2,000 yards in a season. He has coached two different quarterbacks that have recorded 40-plus touchdown pass seasons. Eckley has had three different teams average more than 45 points per game for the season, and has had three teams average more than 500 yards per game in total offense for the season, including the 2007 Union team, which recorded a state record 545 yards per game.

Eckley has also developed four football videos, including videos on quarterback development and the quick passing game. In addition, Eckley has spoken at numerous clinics across the Midwest.

Eckley currently serves as the president of the Missouri Football Coaches Association and is a member of the Football Advisory Committee to MSHSAA, the state's athletics governing body.

Eckley and his wife, Sherene, an elementary teacher, live in Union, Missouri, with their five children, Hannah, Emily, Madison, Hillary, and Marquis.